FOUNDATIONS OF THE
METAPHYSICS OF MORALS

The Library of Liberal Arts
OSKAR PIEST, FOUNDER

FOUNDATIONS OF THE METAPHYSICS OF MORALS
and
WHAT IS ENLIGHTENMENT?

Second Edition, Revised

IMMANUEL KANT

Translated, with an introduction, by
LEWIS WHITE BECK

. . . .

The Library of Liberal Arts
published by

Macmillan Publishing Company
New York
Collier Macmillan Publishers
London

Immanuel Kant: 1724–1804

GRUNDLEGUNG ZUR METAPHYSIK DER SITTEN was originally published in 1785

BEANTWORTUNG DER FRAGE: WAS IST AUFKLÄRUNG? was first published in 1784

Macmillan Publishing Company
866 Third Avenue, New York, New York 10022

Collier Macmillan Canada, Inc.

Library of Congress Cataloging-in-Publication Data

Kant, Immanuel, 1724–1804.
  [Grundlegung zur Metaphysik der Sitten. English]
  Foundations of the metaphysics of morals / Immanuel Kant:
 translated, with an introduction by Lewis White Beck.—2nd ed.,
rev.
    p. cm.—(The Library of liberal arts)
  Translation of: Grundlegung zur Metaphysik der Sitten.
  Bibliography: p.
  ISBN 0-02-307825-1
  1. Ethics. I. Title. II. Series: Library of liberal arts
(Macmillan Publishing Company)
B2766.E6B4 1990
170--dc19   89-2736
            CIP

Printing: 1 2 3 4 5 6 7   Year: 0 1 2 3 4 5 6

 CONTENTS

 TRANSLATOR'S INTRODUCTION

I

Grundlegung zur Metaphysik der Sitten, published in 1785, is one of the most important ethical treatises ever written. Unlike most of Kant's other works, it does not presuppose any knowledge of his *Critique of Pure Reason*, and it is a vivid refutation of the common view that Kant is always obscure, dry, and difficult. It is an eminently suitable introduction to moral philosophy and to the philosophy of Kant as a whole. But unlike some introductions, it is not a work to be read and then put aside for weightier things; like all classics it reveals more on each reading. H. J. Paton called it "one of the small books which are truly great: it has exercised on human thought an influence almost ludicrously disproportionate to its size".[1]

The *Foundations* is for the general reader who possesses common sense knowledge of morality, but lacks a philosophical theory of it. In most cases, the ordinary person knows very well what he or she should do, but is not able to give a philosophical defense of this knowledge. Hence Kant begins with commonly held humanistic ideals of Western civilization, in which there are significant elements from Christianity, Judaism, and Stoic and Platonic philosophy. He examines these ideals to determine their philosophical presuppositions so that he can construct a system of morality based on a new formula, the categorical imperative. When criticized for giving, in this book, only a new formula for some old ways of thinking and acting, he replied: "Who would want to intro-

---

[1] H. J. Paton, in the Preface to his translation of the *Foundations*, published as *The Moral Law, or Kant's Groundwork of the Metaphysics of Morals* (London, 1949).

duce a new principle of morality and, as it were, be its inventor, as if the world had hitherto been ignorant of what duty is, or had been thoroughly wrong about it?"[2]

We must take the title of the book very literally. It is a study of *foundations*, not a complete system of ethics. Kant is not writing casuistry, delineating each right and duty; he is looking for "axioms" that can be used in constructing a general system of morality. Metaphysics, as Kant uses the word here, is not speculation concerning ultimate reality but a rigorous study of moral laws and concepts (such as duty, good, and evil) which, unlike the laws and concepts of psychology, cannot be derived from observation of actual behavior of human beings but require to be established, if at all, by reason. In the light of the fifth paragraph of the Preface, we might paraphrase the title of the book: it could well be called *Foundations of Ethics based upon Reason*.

In the opening sentence of the First Section, Kant says that there is nothing in or out of the world (i.e., nothing either human or divine) that is an unqualified good except a *good will*. However much we may desire happiness and esteem traits of character and enjoy the gifts of fortune that help us in our pursuit of happiness, we do not attribute an unqualified value to happiness and the ways of attaining it. A "rational impartial observer" cannot approve of "a being adorned with no feature of a pure and good will enjoying lasting good fortune" (p. 9). Although being good is not a sure way to happiness—happiness depends not only on character but also on circumstances—it is a condition of *worthiness* to be happy. This belief here embraced by Kant is an essential part of major ethical and religious traditions.

Ordinary people are very well aware of the difference between being good and being cunning in the pursuit of their purposes, and though by nature they desire to be happy, they do not ordinarily think that morality is *merely* a means to happiness (though they may think that being moral is likely in the long run to produce it). It is sometimes said that Kant

[2]Kant, *Critique of Practical Reason*, Preface, n. 5.

believed that a moral act cannot be an act we are glad to do. But this conception of Kant's teaching is a misconception. Kant does not despise success or hold prosperity in contempt or think that happiness is of no importance; he insisted only that our desires and wishes have no standing and are sometimes obstacles that we must try to set aside when it is a question of deciding what we *ought* to do.

Kant is neither an ascetic nor a Pharisee; he is, rather, I believe, describing, in rather stark terms, the ordinary person's conception of the difference between *what we want to do* and *what we ought to do*—even though this same ordinary person (and we are all ordinary in this respect) often chooses to do the former while making it appear (even to him- or herself) that he or she is doing the latter.

Kant elicits from this common sense moral knowledge the principles stated on p. xi. Paraphrased for the sake of clarity, they are:

1. To have genuine moral worth, an action must be done *from duty* (or *for the sake of duty*). (A distinction must be drawn between *a duty*, which is an action that one is obligated to do, and *from duty*, which refers to the motive of the act and which might best be called *dutifulness*).
2. An action performed from duty has its moral worth in the motive of dutifulness and not in the consequences of the action. (Kant's ethics is an ethics of *motive*, only derivatively an ethics of *intention*, and not at all a *consequentialist* ethics.)
3. Duty (in the sense of dutifulness) is the constraint to do an act (a duty) out of respect for a moral law.

Kant believes that the ordinary person, once he or she reflects upon personal moral experience, will come to these conclusions. In one important respect, however, Kant differs from the common person and from many philosophers. Although he thinks, with them, that actions done from sympathy or amiable human nature or even from prudence and (sometimes) ambition may be the right actions in the sense of showing desirable traits of character and having desired consequences, he believes that these same actions can have what he calls *genuine moral worth* if and only if their motive is that of dutifulness to the commands of moral law (Principle 1).

Whether Kant is correct or incorrect in this, his central teaching, will have to be decided by each reader, and it is certainly a matter on which there is no unanimous agreement among moral philosophers. Before you decide that Kant is hopelessly wrong, you should first make sure that you correctly understand his position—a position easy to travesty. This requires a careful examination of Kant's four examples of moral problem solving (pp. 38–40).

In each example, Kant depicts a person doing a right action (e.g., helping others in distress, repaying a loan, developing one's own talents, and renouncing suicide as a way out of misery) even though all the person's desires are against doing the action in question, and only the moral motive of dutifulness is left to influence his or her decision. This has created the impression that for Kant a moral act must always be one that a person does *not* want to do, so that doing the morally right thing makes life unhappy.

This interpretation of the examples misses their point. They are not examples to be imitated but are rather a kind of thought-experiment to show that the identification of the morally correct action is different from the identification of the action that has the consequences we desire. There is this difference even when, as often happens, the action we ought to do is the same as the action we want to do, but the difference is clearer in Kant's examples where the actions are different and opposed to one another. Kant thinks that his examples show (1) that a sense of duty is able to determine our action even when in conflict with our desires and wants, and (2) that the moral action has its genuine moral value from its motive in dutifulness and not from its consequences, no matter how desirable they might be.

Even if it were the case that all human beings tacitly or overtly believe in the correctness of Kant's analysis of moral decision making, they would be far from agreeing in many specific cases on what should be done. They will agree that they should do their duty—but what is their duty? They will agree that they should obey the moral law—but what is the moral law?

The determination of what this law is and what it prescribes is a task of reason. Only pure reason can decide what is an absolutely universal law, permitting no exceptions. An analogy will make this clear.

We cannot have a science of geometry if we merely describe figures drawn on a blackboard; for then we could not say, "All plane triangles have the sum of their internal angles equal to two right angles." Yet we can say this without measuring any triangle. Similarly, we could not say, as we do, that "All persons ought in all cases to treat human beings as ends in themselves," if ethics were merely descriptive of how human beings actually behave. Yet, in geometry and in ordinary moral concern, we enunciate such universal judgments. Since in neither case can these universal judgments or laws be derived by induction from observations of human behavior they must, Kant believes, come from some nonempirical activity of thought, which he calls "pure reason." The system of such judgments is what Kant calls metaphysics, and metaphysics of morals will be the system of such principles of conduct; it will be, as mentioned earlier, ethics based on pure reason.

II

The laying of the foundations of the metaphysics of morals occupies Kant in the Second Section.[3] He tells us again, in the first ten paragraphs, why pure ethics cannot merely describe the way we actually behave, and here and in the closing paragraphs of the section, he criticizes other philosophers who have based their ethics on such a description. The constructive part of the work is found in the intervening para-

[3]Actually the construction is begun, in a tentative way, in the First Section, p. 18.

graphs running from pages 29 to 59. We may divide the construction into five steps.

1. The will is practical reason (p. 29). Whereas all things in nature work "according to laws," a rational being is one who can govern his or her behavior by a *conception* of laws.[4] "Will" is the name generally given (and not by Kant only) to this ground or discipline of action. The judgment to which we refer in deciding on our action is an imperative, a command to act on a certain maxim or motive.

2. An imperative is hypothetical (i.e., it has an "if clause") if it states that some action is right or advisable or necessary as a means to some specific goal. Such an imperative says, "If you would accomplish such and such a goal, you ought to do so and so." An imperative of this kind comes from our experience of the ways in which we may best satisfy our desires; it does not come from pure reason. Hence it does not "command," as a moral imperative does, but only "counsels" us to some line of action. If the goal is some specific object of desire, it cannot be supposed to be universally held by all people or even by myself at all times; hence the hypothetical imperative is conditional upon circumstances and needs.

Even if the goal is happiness, which we may correctly suppose to be desired by all people, we still cannot formulate any universal hypothetical imperatives, for "happiness" is a word of such variable meaning from person to person and from moment to moment that I cannot infer that all people should behave in the same way in order to attain it. Obviously, then, such hypothetical imperatives as we do make have not the status of peremptory and inexorable moral laws. If there is a binding moral law, as Kant believes, it cannot correspond to a hypothetical imperative.

3. A moral imperative is unconditional, i.e., categorical.

---

[4]For example, all unsupported bodies move according to Galileo's law. A rational being, knowing that law (or at least the truth it contains), will refrain from stepping off a high place. The rational being, therefore, acts according to his or her *conception* of a law instead of, like a ball rolling down an inclined plane, moving according to the law itself.

Such an imperative, which seems to be involved in the moral consciousness that we ought to do our duty instead of following our inclinations, cannot, as we have seen, be derived from a psychological study of what our wants and their goals are. If there is such an imperative, it must be formulated by pure reason. If, as in the case before us, no specific goal or condition is stated under which an action is commanded, we must find a formula of the *ought* from the mere concept of *ought* (p. 37): that is, the idea of obligation itself must furnish us a criterion for deciding what our obligations are.

A moral imperative commands unconditional conformity of our maxims to law,[5] but the law contains no reference to specific goals on which it depends. Since we have, in the examples, taken away the contents of the maxims (the wants and desires of the persons), nothing is left to be determined by the law except the form of the maxim; its form must be such as to exclude any contents that would prevent the maxim from itself being universal, i.e., valid for all persons as rational beings regardless of their specific desires. The maxim must, in effect, be capable of being itself a universal law for all rational beings. Thus, we have a test for deciding whether a maxim is conformable to the moral law; Is it a maxim that a rational being could consistently will to be a maxim for all rational beings? The criterion for deciding whether a maxim is moral is the categorical imperative: "Act only according to that maxim by which you can at the same time will that it should become a universal law."

4. There follows a derivation of other formulae of this

---

[5]Kant defines a maxim as the subjective principle of volitions (p. 37, n. 1). He does not mean maxim in the sense of some moralistic commonplace like "Early to bed and early to rise . . ." or "To thine own self be true; and it must follow as the night the day. . . .", but rather a lasting disposition or motive (and its verbal expression) such as "Out of patriotism . . ." or "Out of love for nature," I do the things I do. My maxims will generally be different from yours. Kant's problem is, is there any maxim that ought to be effective in the conduct of *all* rational beings, and if so what is it?

imperative. The first (p. 38) requires that the maxim be fit to be a law of nature, where nature is considered as a harmonious, organic whole. The second (p. 46) is based on the notion that all actions have ends. Are there any ends that we ought to set before ourselves as valid for ourselves and for all human beings regardless of specific personal aims? The answer is that men and women are ends in themselves, and no maxim that does not entail respect for men and women can be a moral law valid for them all. The third (p. 49) requires that we should act in harmony with the idea of the will of every rational being as making universal laws. The fourth (p. 55) requires that the moral agent act as a lawgiving member of a realm of ends, i.e., of persons, each of whom is an end in him- or herself and an end for all others. These are said to be only different formulations of one and the same imperative.

5. From these formulae, there arise two important conceptions: the autonomy of the will and the dignity of the person (pp. 50, 52). In all previous attempts to discover the moral law, it was assumed that there had to be some quid pro quo for morality; hence all imperatives were regarded as hypothetical and every person as having his or her price. But the moral law can obligate unconditionally only if it is a law given by men and women as sovereigns in the realm of ends to themselves as subjects in this realm. In this conception man and woman have the dignity of lawgivers, and do not have to be induced by fear of punishment or hope of reward to obey a law; the laws they obey are the laws they, as purely rational beings, give themselves as beings endowed with reason but affected by desires and emotions. A being who gives the law to him- or herself is not merely bound to the law, but freely bound to it by his or her own lawgiving activity. This is what Kant means by calling the moral will *autonomous*. A person who takes the law from some other lawgiver (God, a tyrant, his or her own cupidity, etc.) must be driven to obedience by hope or fear; that person is not free but *heteronomous*. That person is not truly moral, because all his or her imperatives are hypothetical, and he or she does not act out of respect for a universal law that stands above the partial and conflicting interests of individuals.

III

In spite of its title, the Third Section deals with questions that are likely nowadays to be considered metaphysical, Heretofore Kant's question has been: What is morality, such that we could say, "An action having such and such characteristics would be a moral action"? This is very different from the new question: Can a moral action, so described, actually be performed by a human being? The new question is equivalent to the question: Is the will free? If it is not, then morality is impossible, because in that case the will would be determined by causes foreign to it, and its imperatives would be hypothetical. To show that his ethics based on reason is more than a figment of the imagination, therefore, Kant must show that the will is free to obey the categorical imperative.

Since morality and freedom are cognate or correlative concepts (i.e., concepts mutually implicative of each other, like "husband" and "wife"), we cannot use one concept to establish the *reality* of the other. Any argument that we must be free because we are morally obligated, or the converse, is a *petitio principii* (p. 67) since "morally obligated" means "subject to a categorical imperative" and "free" (in this statement) also means autonomous, "subject to a categorical imperative." Nevertheless the close logical connection between freedom and morality furnishes us with a third conception, which will permit us to break out of the vicious circle. At the end of the second paragraph Kant promises us this third conception, which is finally formulated in the third paragraph ending on p. 70.

To find a way out of this circle, Kant gives us, on pp. 69 to 72, a rapid survey of some of the conclusions of the *Critique of Pure Reason* and the *Prolegomena to Any Future Metaphysics*. All that we perceive, he tells us, is only appearance, how things appear to us and not how they are in themselves. These appearances are connected by causal laws discovered by observation and experiment, and the system of these phenomena under laws is what we call the common world of nature (chairs and tables, stars and atoms, human bodies, etc.). We ourselves are parts of nature and hence under laws of causal determination. "Behind" the appearances there is a real world which we don't know; beyond the appearance that we call a human being is "something else as its basis, the ego as it is in itself" (p. 68). Each person ascribes to this ego whatever is pure *activity* in him- or herself, whereas in the world of appearance one sees only *reactivity* to stimuli. This pure activity is reason, and it is manifested, for instance, when I draw a correct inference from premises that are reasons for my conclusion and when I do not just react to psychological or physiological causes. Hence as a reasonable being (reasonable in the sense of being able to think correctly), I may presume myself to be free, though as an animal I am under the mechanism of nature. Thus we have reason to believe human beings are free, regardless of whether in fact they are or may be moral.

Kant thinks the circle in the argument has thus been broken. He has shown, quite apart from moral considerations, that man and woman must conceive of themselves as "above nature" and to this extent as free from its causal laws; yet they can be seen also as a part of nature and, as such, not free. In their former role, as what they really are, they give a law to themselves in their latter role, as what they only appear to be. The self as free supersensuous reality gives a law to the self as a causally determined appearance. The sought-for proposition that permits us to break out of the circle is: "If we think of ourselves as free [even in a nonmoral context], we transport ourselves into the intelligible world as members of it and know the autonomy of the will together with its consequence, morality; whereas if we think of ourselves as obligated, we consider ourselves as belonging both to the world of sense and at the same time to the intelligible world" (p. 70).

Philosophy cannot establish any knowledge of this supersensible world in which we are citizens and lawgivers. Philosophy's task, as Kant conceives it, is to point out that freedom is possible, and to mark out a region that fatalistic and materialistic speculation cannot invade so as to destroy the foundations of morality (p. 74). In the words of the *Critique of Pure Reason*, Kant "found it necessary to deny knowledge [of the supersensible world] in order to make room for faith. The dogmatism of metaphysics . . . is the source of all that unbelief [in the presuppositions of morality], itself always very dogmatic, which wars against morality."[6] Philosophy cannot render the freedom of the will comprehensible, but it can show why it is incomprehensible (p. 82).

Kant here seems to be committing himself to Platonism. In both philosophies there seems to be a duality of worlds, the world of space and time and appearances, and the world of things in themselves conceived by pure reason alone. (*Noumena* is the name both Plato and Kant use to refer to objects of thought not in the world of appearances and images.) For both philosophers the conception of the intelligible world is a law for the phenomenal world. "In the heavens," says Plato, "there is laid up a pattern of [the ideal moral commonwealth] which he who desires may behold, and beholding, he may set his own house in order."[7] And a disciple of Kant wrote similarly: "Just because reason cannot find its ideal realized in the world [of phenomena], it seeks to realize that ideal for itself."[8]

But Kant's Platonism is strangely inverted. For Plato, the intelligible world was the object of the highest form of knowledge, and the knowledge of the empirical world was of a lower order, like a glass seen through darkly. For Kant, our knowledge is confined within boundaries of possible experience; it is the noumenal world that is not known, but is only an object of thought and rational (not religious) faith.

The history of philosophy has made the difficulties of any two-world theory well known. In recent years there have been efforts to interpret Kant as holding the theory that there are two aspects of things: the noumenal aspect, the object regarded as an object of pure thought, and the phenomenal aspect: the very same object seen from the point of view of a being endowed like us with sense organs as well as the power

[6]*Critique of Pure Reason*, Preface to second edition. p. xxx, trans. by Norman Kemp Smith (London, 1923), p. 29.

[7]Plato, *The Republic*, end of Book ix.

[8]Edward Caird, *The Critical Philosophy of Immanuel Kant*, II, 164.

of pure reason. In one aspect, as presented to thought, human beings are free noumenal agents; in another aspect, as presented to observation and scientific scrutiny by psychologists and physiologists, human beings are parts of the mechanism of nature in which there is no place for value, purpose, or freedom.[9] Ordinarily we shift back and forth from one point of view to the other, and since we don't occupy two standpoints at the same time, we minimize the apparent incompatibility between them. Whether we judge human beings to be free or to be mechanically determined, to be subject to moral judgment or to be exempt from it, depends not so much on a metaphysical dualism of two selves in two worlds as on a duality of perspectives from which we view a single common subject. The perspective we take is determined by the nature of our concern — are we interested in giving a causal explanation of a person's behavior, perhaps in the hope that we can foretell that person's future actions? Or are we interested in judging the character of his or her actions so that we know whether to impute moral responsibility to the person?

Whether this two-aspect theory avoids the difficulties of the two-world theory and whether it is encumbered with fatal difficulties of its own remain to be seen. The topic is in the center of much contemporary debate among Kant scholars and other philosophers, and the verdict is not yet in.[10]

IV

I shall here consider a few common criticisms of Kant's ethics often considered fatal to his theory, but in fact based on patent and widespread misinterpretations of it.

1. *Kant's ethics is "empty," because the categorical imper-*

---

[9]For a presentation of this point of view, see B. F. Skinner, *Beyond Freedom and Dignity* (1971).

[10]The first major presentation of the two-aspect theory, and perhaps still the best, is in H. J. Paton's *The Categorical Imperative* (Chicago, 1948), ch. 22.

ative does not have any definite implications for action. This reveals a misunderstanding of the function of the imperative. It is a rule like the rule of a syllogism, and just as the rules of syllogism are empty but tell us what premises are logically necessary in drawing a specific conclusion, or what conclusions follow from given premises, the categorical imperative is a rule for determining what maxims are relevant in making moral decision. The criticism assumes that the categorical imperative is a premise from which specific conclusions ought to be drawn; but no specific conclusions can be drawn from it any more that they can be drawn merely from the rules of syllogism. In each case, premises or actual maxims have to be used, and the rules of logic and of ethics tell us which can be properly used or what their conclusion must be. The categorical imperative is not and was not meant to be a casuistical principle or an axiom from which moral decisions could be drawn as it were *in vacuo.*[11]

2. *Kant's ethics is trivial, and does not discriminate between moral and merely permissible actions.* For, it is said, I can make many maxims universal without rendering them moral. For instance, I have the policy of writing my name on the flyleaf of each of my books, and I can consistently will that all people should write their names in their books, but this does not mean that I have a moral obligation to write my name in my books. This criticism, however, overlooks the fact that Kant carefully distinguishes between actions that *conform to* a law (which he calls "legal actions") and those done *because of* a law (moral actions proper). I do not write my name in my books because I can will that all other people should do so; I do it so that my books will not be lost. In a genuinely moral action, however, I decide what I ought to do by finding out what I would will that every rational being should do. Kant asserts that in moral action there are not two volitions (what I will for myself and what I will for others),

---

[11]An excellent discussion of this objection is to be found in Onora Nell's *Acting on Principle. An Essay on Kantian Ethics* (New York, 1975).

but only one volition. The moral imperative is: "Never choose except in such a way that the maxims of the choice are comprehended *in the same volition* as a universal law" (p. 57, italics added). That is, I am obliged to do a moral act because I cannot consistently will that all rational beings should act in one way and yet make an exception of myself.

3. *Kant minimizes the role of practical intelligence in life, and instead of calling for more facts and acknowledging the problematic and tentative character of most of our difficult decisions, he requires us only to apply mechanically a simple logical rule.* As in so many of these objections, there is a kernel of truth. Kant repeatedly talks about how much intelligence and investigation are needed if we are to be prudent and skillful in attaining our ends. By contrast, he often oversimplifies making a moral decision, and says "I do not need any penetrating acuteness in order to discern what I have to do" when it is a matter of morality and not of mere prudence (p. 19). In the simple cases Kant uses as examples this may be true, but in real life where duties seem to conflict with each other (and not just with our passions and wishes) things are not so simple.

Kant does not deny the need for facts in making decisions, but the question is, what facts are relevant if the decision is moral? Some facts (e.g., the color of a person's skin) *ought not* to figure in a moral decision about that person's rights. Kant gives a rule for deciding what facts are relevant: we must determine what facts a rational being would consistently take into account in willing that his or her maxim should be operative also in other people.

4. *Kant's theory is not "true to human nature"; Kant requires human beings to be more rational than they can be.* Certainly Kant is not an irrationalist who believes that reason is only a kind of rationalization of our emotions. He insists on the moral struggle that is sometimes necessary to bring our emotions and passions under rational control. "Virtue," he says, "is the moral disposition in conflict." He admits that man is not completely rational, but he also insists, in a way reminiscent of Aristotle and in many ways anticipating John

Dewey, that morality is conduct guided by reason. But reason is never claimed to be all-powerful, and Kant is, in fact, rather more pessimistic about human rational competence than either Aristotle or Dewey.

5. *Kant's ethics is one-sided because he despised the emotions.* This criticism arises from the fact that Kant is usually arguing against philosophers who thought the emotions were primary and sufficient for morality; the result is that he emphasizes the role of reason and often seems to neglect the emotions. If we read Kant with this polemical situation in mind, it will not surprise us that he did not emphasize the emotional though he was still aware of it and its place in conduct. Besides, the proper place to stress the emotions is not in a book on the ethics of *pure reason*; when it is not out of place in other books Kant is ready to accept the emotional component of moral virtue. For instance, in response to this same criticism by the poet Friedrich Schiller, Kant spoke of "a joyous state of mind without which man is never certain of having really attained a love for the good, i.e., of having incorporated it into his maxim."[12]

6. *Kantian ethics may be good in theory but would not work in practice; rather, it would have catastrophic consequences. But, of course, consequences did not count with Kant.* The argument goes like this: An action is not right for me unless I can will that everyone should do it. I thought it was right for me to eat at the Ritz Hotel at midnight. But if it were right for everyone, and if everyone tried to do it none of us could eat there (or, for that matter, anywhere). Result: starvation.

This objection overlooks the explicit wording of the categorical imperative. It commands us to act from a universalizable maxim, but it does not command everyone to do, under that maxim, the same action. I am willing for everyone to eat at any proper time and place he or she wishes, because my maxim is *laissez aller*, and that maxim *can* be universalized.

---

[12]Kant, *Religion within the Limits of Reason Alone* (trans. by H. H. Hudson and T. M. Greene, New York, 1960), p. 19n.

The objection, however, is not as frivolous as it looks. Sometimes a universalizable maxim can be carried out in hardly more than one way. The maxim of truthfulness can be made effective only by telling the truth. Hence the categorical imperative sometimes in effect commands a specific action. This can lead to a conflict of duties; the duty to tell the truth may conflict with the duty to save the life of an innocent person, a duty that may require misinforming a would-be murderer about where his victim is. Kant deals with such questions in his *Metaphysics of Morals, Lectures on Ethics*, and in the famous (or infamous) essay "On an Alleged Right to Lie from Altruistic Motives." There is a very large amount of writing on Kant as a casuist,[13] and it cannot be said he is superior to many other philosophers in handling cases of conflicting duties.

7. *Kant is "too rigoristic."* "Every law has some exceptions," we are told, and Kant's denial that we should tell a lie even to save the life of an innocent person is taken as a *reductio ad absurdum* of his theory. Kant is himself partly to blame for this criticism, since it is based upon one of this own examples. Yet Kant is not in principle called upon to assert the universality of any particular rule, even that against lying. Rather, the laws Kant insists upon are laws of maxims, not directly of actions. The exceptions that are brought against him are always exceptions to specific rules or kinds of act. One can easily think up legitimate exceptions to rules of action; for instance, although there is a valid rule that one should return what one has borrowed, one need not return a book one has borrowed when there is a heavy snowstorm and the lender is not in immediate need of it. But it is not easy to think of warranted exceptions to moral maxims. When should we make an exception to the maxim that we ought to treat our fellow human beings as ends in themselves and not as means only? When is it morally right to act from selfish motives instead of duteous motives? When we make an exception to a particular rule, we justify the exception by reference to a maxim that, we think, has no exceptions.

[13]See Marcus G. Singer, *Generalization in Ethics* (New York, 1961).

8. *Kant takes a provincial moral code and absolutizes it.*
The same reply can be made to this as to objection (7).
Certainly Kant's examples were taken from his and our traditions and history. But it is not the examples or the specific
precepts that Kant universalized, though since he was dealing
with a highly homogeneous culture he seldom thought to
illustrate his doctrines with reference to examples taken from
savage peoples. What he wanted universalized was the requirement that a certain character be found in all our maxims
regardless of their specific content, which will vary from person to person and culture to culture. He is thus in a better
position than most absolutists (who believe in a single ideal
ethical code for all humankind) to take account of the indisputable facts of cultural relativity, for he had found, he believed, a principle of morality that is a cultural invariant. This
also gives him an answer to the skeptical doubts usually
drawn from the facts of cultural relativity; at the same time he
does not have to be ethnocentric about the moral practices of
Königsberg and try to establish its provincial code of specific
rules as universally binding.

9. *Kant's ethics is an ethics suitable for a totalitarian state
or tyranny: One ought to do one's duty, blindly and unquestioningly, even if the duty is exacted by a ruthless dictator
who commands immoral acts.* If this charge can be sustained,
it is the most serious ground there could be for rejecting
Kant's ethics and rejecting Kant himself as one of the moral
teachers of humankind. This objection has been made many
times, sometimes as a part of raw nationalistic war propaganda, but occasionally by reputable scholars.

Fortunately it is easy to refute the main point of this objection. Kant holds that the duty that morally binds is not a duty
because it is under statute law or an arbitrary decree by a
dictator or tyrant; it is not even a command of God to which I
should be dutifully subservient. The duty he espouses is constraint over our motives by our acknowledgment of the moral
law. We should execute duties that arise in this way, for only
in this way are we both obedient and free, i.e., self-governed.
So far from Kant's philosophy laying the foundations of fascism or totalitarianism, his ethical theory is rather a founda-

tion for a republican form of government in which ultimately the citizens rule themselves by participating in making the laws that they obligate themselves to obey. This is perfectly explicit in Kant's political writings (especially in *Perpetual Peace*). It is no wonder that his books were burned by the Nazis in 1933.

Nevertheless something should be said about Kant himself and his political attitudes. As a professor in Königsberg, he was a civil servant of the Prussian state and a faithful subject of Frederick the Great. As a Lutheran in a Lutheran educational system and culture, he adhered (as a personal orientation perhaps independently of his philosophical theory) to the Lutheran doctrine of the passive obedience we owe to duly constituted authority. Change of government policy, which Kant from time to time ardently promoted, should be brought about gradually by research, publication, and education, not by rebellion.

Yet Kant was an enthusiast for the American and the French revolutions. He defied the Prussian government's decree against his religious teachings. He opposed the repressive forces limiting freedom of the press. He was one of the principal architects of the eighteenth-century doctrine of the inalienable rights of mankind.

This is not the place to try to reconcile these personal ideals of the man Kant. His attitude toward revolution is especially obscure.[14] But suffice it to say that, in his political and ethical writings, he was closer to the authors of the Declaration of Independence, of the Constitution of the United States, and of the Declaration of the Rights of Man and of the Citizen (in the French Revolution) than he was to Hitler and Stalin. *What is Enlightenment?* is a classic defense of intellectual freedom.

---

[14]For clarification of it, see John E. Atwell, *Ends and Principles in Kant's Moral Thought* (Dordrecht, 1986), pp. 174–193.

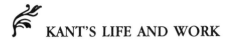 KANT'S LIFE AND WORK

Immanuel Kant was born in Königsberg, East Prussia (now Kaliningrad, USSR), April 22, 1724. His family were Pietists, a Lutheran sect somewhat like the Quakers and early Methodists. Pietism's deeply ethical orientation and singular lack of emphasis on theological dogmatism became a part of Kant's mature nature and a determining factor in his philosophy. After attending the University of Königsberg and serving as tutor in several aristocratic families, Kant became an instructor (*Privatdozent*) at the university. He held this position for fifteen years, lecturing and writing on metaphysics, logic, ethics, mathematics, and the natural sciences. He made significant, but at the time not widely known, contributions to astronomy, being the originator of what is today known as the Kant-La Place nebular hypothesis of the origin of planetary systems.

In 1770 he was appointed Professor of Logic and Metaphysics in Königsberg, and in 1781 he published his most important work, *Critique of Pure Reason*. This opened up new fields of study and problems for him at an age when most men are about ready to retire; but for Kant there followed nearly twenty years of unremitting labor and unparalleled accomplishment. Merely a list of his most important writings published in seventeen years shows this: *Prolegomena to Any Future Metaphysics* (1783), *What Is Enlightenment?* and *Idea for a Universal History* (1784), *Foundation of the Metaphysics of Morals* (1785), *Metaphysical Foundations of Natural Science* (1786), second edition of *Critique of Pure Reason* (1787), *Critique of Practical Reason* (1788), *Critique of Judgment* (1790), *Religion within the Boundaries of Reason Alone* (1793), *Theory and Practice* (1793), *Perpetual Peace* (1795), *Metaphysics of Ethics*, two volumes, (1797), *Anthropology from a Pragmatic Point of View* (1798), and *The Strife of the Faculties* (1798). He died in Königsberg on February 12, 1804.

Kant's personality, or at least a caricature of it, is well known. Most people who know nothing else of Kant do know that the housewives of Königsberg were said to have set their clocks by his afternoon walk. Heinrich Heine said a life of Kant could not be written because Kant had no life. But a truer picture of his personality — less pedantic, Prussian, and puritanical — comes to us from the German writer Johann Gottfried Herder:

> I have had the good fortune to know a philosopher. He was my teacher. In his prime he had the happy sprightliness of a youth; he continued to have it, I believe, even as a very old man. His broad forehead, built for thinking, was the seat of an imperturbable cheerfulness and joy. Speech, the richest in thought, flowed from his lips. Playfulness, wit, and humor were at his command. His lectures were the most entertaining talks; his mind, which examined Leibniz, Wolff, Baumgarten, Crusius, and Hume, and investigated the laws of nature of Newton, Kepler, and the physicists, comprehended equally the newest works of Rousseau . . . and the latest discoveries in science. He weighed them all, and always came back to the unbiased knowledge of nature and to the moral worth of man. The history of men and peoples, natural history and science, mathematics and observation, were the sources from which he enlivened his lectures and conversation. He was indifferent to nothing worth knowing. No cabal, no sect, no prejudice, no desire for fame could ever tempt him in the slightest away from broadening and illuminating the truth. He incited and gently forced others to think for themselves; despotism was foreign to his mind. This man, whom I name with the greatest gratitude and respect, was Immanuel Kant.

NOTE ON THE TEXT

The translation is from *Kants Werke* published by the Royal
Prussian Academy of Sciences. Intentional departures from
this edition are indicated by use of square brackets or, occasionally, by explanatory footnotes. Numbers in the margins
refer to the Academy edition pages; this is the pagination
usually cited in scholarly works on Kant, and these numbers
facilitate use of the secondary literature. Numbered footnotes
are by the editor, Kant's notes being identified by asterisk or
dagger.

The present translations derive from the versions that I first
published in 1949 (University of Chicago Press, reissued with
minor revision from time to time by Chicago, The Library of
Liberal Arts, Bobbs-Merrill, and Macmillan). In 1988 Macmillan published a large anthology, *Kant Selections*, which contained thoroughly revised translations, substantially identical
with those in this volume. Scholars who use my translation of
the two works are requested to cite and quote this edition and
no longer the earlier ones.

Two lexical matters require attention. Kant's word *Vorstellung*, as the generic name for any content of consciousness, is
literally translated as *representation* when verbal exactitude
is very important, and in less formal and technical contexts it
is translated as *conception, thought,* or *idea* (lower case i).
Kant's word *Idee*, when it refers to a pure concept of reason to
which no intuition can be given, is translated as *Idea* (upper
case I); when it is used loosely, it is translated as *idea* (lower
case i). The context almost always makes it clear whether
Kant is using *Vorstellung* and *Idee* in a loose or strict sense.

Kant does not use the expression *Ding an sich* in the *Foundations*, but invariably writes *Ding an sich selbst*. Following
the argument by Gerold Prauss in his *Kant und das Problem
der Dinge an sich* (Bonn, 1974) that the latter expression is

elliptic for *Ding an sich selbst betrachtet,* I have translated it: *the thing regarded as it is in itself,* or, more loosely, *the thing as it is in itself.* The correct interpretation of this in contrast to *thing in itself* has a bearing upon the controversy between the two-world theory and the two-aspect theory (see p. xviii).

 SELECTED BIBLIOGRAPHY

Acton, H. B. *Kant's Moral Philosophy*. London: Macmillan, 1970. The best brief introduction to Kant's ethics.

Aune, Bruce. *Kant's Theory of Morals*. Princeton University Press, 1979. Written in the "analytical idiom," useful in more advanced study.

Beck, Lewis White, *A Commentary on Kant's Critique of Practical Reason*. Chicago: University of Chicago Press, 1960. Chiefly about the second *Critique*, but naturally covers all the principal parts of the *Foundations*.

Duncan, A. R. C. *Practical Reason and Morality. A Study of Immanuel Kant's Foundations for the Metaphysics of Morals*. Edinburgh: Thomas Nelson, 1957. An unusual interpretation, critical of Paton.

Liddell, Brendan E. A. *Kant on the Foundation of Morality. A Modern Version of the Grundlegung*. Bloomington: Indiana University Press, 1970. In part translation, in part commentary. Useful for beginning study.

Paton, H. J. *The Categorical Imperative. A Study in Kant's Moral Philosophy*. Chicago: University of Chicago Press, 1948. Beyond question in the best sympathetic interpretation of Kant's ethical theory.

Ross, Sir David. *Kant's Ethical Theory. A Commentary on the Grundlegung zur Metaphysik der Sitten*. Oxford: Clarendon Press, 1954. Critical, not always accurate.

Scott, John Waugh. *Kant on the Moral Life: An Exposition of Kant's "Grundlegung"*. London: Black, 1924. A simplified exposition, in part paraphrase. Like Liddell's book, useful to those who find Kant's style too difficult.

Sullivan, Roger J. *Immanuel Kant's Moral Theory.* Cambridge University Press, 1989. Probably the most comprehensive study of Kant's ethics as a whole; especially instructive on present-day controversies.

Williams, T. C. *The Concept of the Categorical Imperative. A Study of the Place of the Categorical Imperative in Kant's Ethical Theory.* Oxford: Clarendon Press, 1968. An interesting effort to reconcile Paton's and Duncan's interpretation of the *Foundations*; gives major emphasis to the intuitionistic element in Kant's ethics.

Wolff, Robert Paul. *The Autonomy of Reason. A Commentary on Kant's Groundwork of the Metaphysics of Morals.* New York: Harper Torchbooks, 1973. Deals mostly with the problem of freedom and the two-world theory.

Wolff, Robert Paul, ed. *Kant. Foundations of the Metaphysics of Morals. Text and Critical Essays.* New York: Bobbs-Merrill, 1969. An earlier version of the Beck translation with nine critical essays on important topics in the *Foundations*.

FOUNDATIONS OF THE
METAPHYSICS OF MORALS

FOUNDATIONS OF THE METAPHYSICS
OF MORALS

Preface

Ancient Greek philosophy was divided into three sciences: physics, ethics, and logic. This division conforms perfectly to the nature of the subject, and one need improve on it perhaps only by supplying its principle in order both to insure its exhaustiveness and to define correctly the necessary subdivisions.

All rational knowledge is either material, and concerns some object, or formal, and is occupied only with the form of understanding and reason itself and with the universal rules of thinking, without regard to distinctions among objects. Formal philosophy is called logic. Material philosophy, however, which has to do with definite objects and the laws to which they are subject, is divided into two parts. This is because these laws are either laws of nature or laws of freedom. The science of the former is called physics, and that of the latter ethics. The former is also called theory of nature and the latter theory of morals.

Logic can have no empirical part—a part in which universal and necessary laws of thinking would rest upon grounds taken from experience. For in that case it would not be logic (i.e., a canon for understanding or reason which is valid for all thinking and which must be demonstrated). Natural and moral philosophy, on the other hand, can each have its empirical part. The former must do so, for it must determine the laws of nature as an object of experience, and the latter must do so because it must determine the human will so far as it is affected by nature. The laws of the former are laws according to which everything happens; those of the latter are laws according to which everything ought to happen, but allow for conditions under which what ought to happen often does not.

All philosophy, so far as it is based on experience, may be called empirical; but, so far as it presents its doctrines solely on the basis of a priori principles, it may be called pure philosophy. Pure philosophy, when formal only, is logic; when limited to definite objects of the understanding, it is metaphysics.

In this way there arises the idea of a two-fold metaphysics —a metaphysics of nature and a metaphysics of morals. Physics, therefore, will have an empirical part and also a rational part, and ethics likewise. In ethics, however, the empirical part may be called more specifically practical anthropology; the rational part, morals proper.

All crafts, handiworks, and arts have gained by the division of labor, for when one person does not do everything but each limits himself to a particular job which is distinguished from all the others by the treatment it requires, he can do it with greater perfection and more facility. Where work is not thus differentiated and divided, where everyone is a jack-of-all-trades, the crafts remain at a primitive level. It might be worth considering whether pure philosophy in each of its parts does not require a man particularly devoted to it, and whether it would not be better for the learned profession as a whole to warn those who are in the habit of catering to the taste of the public by mixing up the empirical with the rational in all sorts of proportions which they themselves do not know—a warning to those who call themselves independent thinkers and who give the name of speculator to those who apply themselves exclusively to the rational part of philosophy. This warning would be that they should not, at one and the same time, carry on two employments which differ widely in the treatment they require, and for each of which perhaps a special talent is required, since the combination of these talents in one person produces only bunglers. I only ask whether the nature of the science does not require that a careful separation of the empirical from the rational part be made, with a metaphysics of nature put before real (empirical) physics and a metaphysics of morals before practical anthropology. Each branch of metaphysics must be carefully purified of everything empirical so that we can know how much pure reason can accomplish in each case and from what sources it creates its a priori teaching, whether the latter 389 inquiry be conducted by all moralists (whose name is legion) or only by some who feel a calling to it.

Since my purpose here is directed to moral philosophy, I narrow my proposed question to this: Is it not of the utmost necessity to construct a pure moral philosophy which is completely freed from everything which may be only empirical and thus belong to anthropology? That there must be such a philosophy is self-evident from the common idea of duty and moral laws. Everyone must admit that a law, if it is to hold morally (i.e., as a ground of obligation), must imply absolute necessity; he must admit that the command: Thou shalt not lie, does not apply to men only as if other rational beings had no need to observe it. The same is true for all other moral laws properly so called. He must concede that the ground of obligation here must not be sought in the nature of man or in the circumstances in which he is placed but a priori solely in the concepts of pure reason, and that every precept which rests on principles of mere experience, even a precept which is in certain respects universal, so far as it leans in the least on empirical grounds (perhaps only in regard to the motive involved) may be called a practical rule but never a moral law.

Thus not only are moral laws together with their principles essentially different from all practical knowledge in which there is anything empirical, but all moral philosophy rests solely on its pure part. Applied to man, it borrows nothing from knowledge of him (anthropology) but gives man, as a rational being, a priori laws. No doubt these laws require a power of judgment sharpened by experience partly in order to decide in which cases they apply and partly to procure for them access to man's will and to provide an impetus to their practice. For man is affected by so many inclinations that, though he is capable of the Idea of a practical pure reason, he is not so easily able to make it concretely effective in the conduct of his life.

A metaphysics of morals is therefore indispensable, not
390   merely because of motives to speculation on the source of the
a priori practical principles which lie in our reason, but also
because morals themselves remain subject to all kinds of
corruption so long as the guide and supreme norm for their
correct estimation is lacking. For it is not sufficient to that
which should be morally good that it conform to the law; it
must be done for the sake of the law. Otherwise its conformity is merely contingent and spurious because, though the
unmoral ground may indeed now and then produce lawful
actions, more often it brings forth unlawful ones. But the
moral law can be found in its purity and genuineness (which
is the central concern in the practical) nowhere else than in a
pure philosophy; therefore metaphysics must lead the way,
and without it there can be no moral philosophy. Philosophy
which mixes pure principles with empirical ones does not
deserve the name, for what distinguishes philosophy from
common sense knowledge is its treatment in separate
sciences of what is confusedly apprehended in such knowledge. Much less does it deserve the name of moral philosophy, since by this confusion it spoils the purity of morals
themselves, and works contrary to its own end.

It should not be thought that what is here required is
already present in the celebrated Wolff's propaedeutic to his
moral philosophy (i.e., in what he calls *Universal Practical
Philosophy*) and that it is not an entirely new field which is to
be opened. Precisely because his work was to be universal
practical philosophy, it contained no will of any particular
kind, such as one determined without any empirical motives
by a priori principles; in a word, it had nothing which could
be called a pure will, since it considered only volition in
general with all the actions and conditions which pertain to it
in this general sense. Thus his propaedeutic differs from a
metaphysic of morals in the same way that general logic is
distinguished from transcendental philosophy, the former ex-
pounding the actions and rules of thinking in general, and the
latter presenting the actions and rules of pure thinking (thinking by which objects are known completely a priori). For the

metaphysics of morals is meant to investigate the Idea and principles of a possible pure will and not the actions and conditions of human volition as such, which for the most part are drawn from psychology.

That universal practical philosophy discussed (though im- 391 properly) laws and duty is no objection to my assertion. For the authors of this science remain even here true to their idea of it. They do not distinguish the motives which are presented completely a priori by reason alone and which are thus moral in the proper sense of the world, from empirical motives which the understanding raises to universal concepts by comparing experiences. Rather, they consider motives without regard to the difference in their source but only with reference to their larger or smaller number (as they are considered to be all of the same kind); they thus formulate their concept of obligation, which is anything but moral, but which is all that can be desired in a philosophy which does not decide whether the origin of all possible practical concepts is a priori or a posteriori.

As a preliminary to a *Metaphysics of Morals* which I intend to publish someday, I issue these *Foundations*. There is, to be sure, no other foundation for such a metaphysics than a critical examination of pure practical reason, just as there is no other foundation for metaphysics than the already published critical examination of pure speculative reason. But, in the first place, a critical examination of pure practical reason is not of such extreme importance as that of the speculative reason, because human reason, even in the commonest mind, can easily be brought to a high degree of correctness and completeness in moral matters while, on the other hand, in its theoretical but pure use it is wholly dialectical. In the second place, I require of a critical examination of pure practical reason, if it is to be complete, that its unity with the speculative be subject to presentation under a common principle, because in the final analysis there can be but one and the same reason which must be different only in application. But I could not bring this to such a completeness without bringing in observations of an altogether different kind and without thereby confusing the reader. For these reasons I have employed the title, *Foundations of the Metaphysics of Morals,* instead of *Critique of Pure Practical Reason.*

Because, in the third place, a *Metaphysics of Morals,* in spite of its forbidding title, is capable of a high degree of popular adaptation to common understanding, I find it useful to separate this preliminary work of laying the foundation, in order not to have to introduce unavoidable subtleties into the latter, more comprehensible work.

392

The present foundations, however, are nothing more than the search for and establishment of the supreme principle of morality. This constitutes a task altogether complete in design and one which should be kept separate from all other moral inquiry. My conclusions concerning this important question, which has not yet been discussed nearly enough, would, of course, be clarified by application of the principle to the whole system of morality, and it would receive much confirmation by the adequacy which it would everywhere show. But I must forego this advantage which would be, in the final analysis, more personally gratifying than commonly useful, because ease of use and apparent adequacy of a principle are not any sure proof of correctness, but rather awaken a certain partiality which prevents a rigorous investigation and evaluation of it for itself without regard to consequences.

I have adopted in this writing the method which is, I think, most suitable if one wishes to proceed analytically from common knowledge to the determination of its supreme principle, and then synthetically from the examination of this principle and its sources back to common knowledge where it finds its application. The division is therefore as follows:

1. First Section. Transition from Common Sense Knowledge of Morals to the Philosophical
2. Second Section. Transition from Popular Moral Philosophy to the Metaphysics of Morals
3. Third Section. Final Step from the Metaphysics of Morals to the Critical Examination of Pure Practical Reason

First Section
Transition from Common Sense[1] Knowledge of Morals to the Philosophical

Nothing in the world—indeed nothing even beyond the 393
world—can possibly be conceived which could be called
good without qualification except a *GOOD WILL*. Intelligence, wit, judgment, and other talents of the mind however
they may be named, or courage, resoluteness, and persever-
ence as qualities of temperament, are doubtless in many respects good and desirable; but they can become extremely
bad and harmful if the will, which is to make use of these gifts
of nature and which in its special constitution is called character, is not good. It is the same with gifts of fortune. Power,
riches, honor, even health, general well-being and the contentment with one's condition which is called happiness
make for pride and even arrogance if there is not a good will
to correct their influence on the mind and on its principle of
action, so as to make it generally fitting to its entire end. It
need hardly be mentioned that the sight of a being adorned
with no feature of a pure and good will yet enjoying lasting
good fortune can never give pleasure to an impartial rational
observer. Thus the good will seems to constitute the indispensable condition even of worthiness to be happy.

Some qualities seem to be conducive to this good will and
can facilitate its action, but in spite of that they have no
intrinsic unconditional worth. They rather presuppose a good 394
will, which limits the high esteem which one otherwise

---

[1]*gemeine Vernunfterkenntnis* (common rational knowledge) is one
of several expressions Kant uses which may sometimes best be translated as "common sense." See p. 18. Kant is very strict in his censure of
those who appeal to common sense as an arbiter in philosophical dis-
putes, yet he accepts it as a starting point, especially in ethics, where he
says that the man of common sense has a least as much chance to be
right as the philosopher (p. 20). In this title "common sense" is not
being used as a technical term; it just means "what everyone knows"
about morality.

rightly has for them and prevents their being held to be absolutely good. Moderation in emotions and passions, self-control, and calm deliberation not only are good in many respects but seem even to constitute part of the inner worth of the person. But however unconditionally they were esteemed by the ancients, they are far from being good without qualification, for without the principles of a good will they can become extremely bad, and the coolness of a villain makes him not only far more dangerous but also more directly abominable in our eyes than he would have seemed without it.

The good will is not good because of what it effects or accomplishes or because of its competence to achieve some intended end; it is good only because of its willing (i.e., it is good in itself). And, regarded for itself, it is to be esteemed as incomparably higher than anything which could be brought about by it in favor of any inclination or even of the sum total of all inclinations. Even if it should happen that, by a particularly unfortunate fate or by the niggardly provision of a stepmotherly nature, this will should be wholly lacking in power to accomplish its purpose, and if even the greatest effort should not avail it to achieve anything of its end, and if there remained only the good will — not as a mere wish, but as the summoning of all the means in our power — it would sparkle like a jewel all by itself, as something that had its full worth in itself. Usefulness or fruitlessness can neither diminish nor augment this worth. Its usefulness would be only its setting, as it were, so as to enable us to handle it more conveniently in commerce or to attract the attention of those who are not yet connoisseurs, but not to recommend it to those who are experts or to determine its worth.

But there is something so strange in this idea of the absolute worth of the will alone, in which no account is taken of any use, that, notwithstanding the agreement even of common sense, the suspicion must arise that perhaps only high-flown fancy is its hidden basis, and that we may have misunderstood the purpose of nature in appointing reason as the ruler of our will. We shall therefore examine this idea from this point of view.

395

In the natural constitution of an organized being (i.e., one suitably adapted to life), we assume as an axiom that no organ will be found for any purpose which is not the fittest and best adapted to that purpose. Now if its preservation, its welfare, in a word its happiness, were the real end of nature in a being having reason and will, then nature would have hit upon a very poor arrangement in appointing the reason of the creature to be the executor of this purpose. For all the actions which the creature has to perform with this intention of nature, and the entire rule of his conduct, would be dictated much more exactly by instinct, and the end would be far more certainly attained by instinct than it ever could be by reason. And if, over and above this, reason should have been granted to the favored creature, it would have served only to let him contemplate the happy constitution of his nature, to admire it, to rejoice in it, and to be grateful for it to its beneficent cause. But reason would not have been given in order that the being should subject his faculty of desire to that weak and delusive guidance and to meddle with the purpose of nature. In a word, nature would have taken care that reason did not break forth into practical use nor have the presumption, with its weak insight, to think out for itself the plan of happiness and the means of attaining it. Nature would have taken over the choice not only of ends but also of the means, and with wise foresight she would have entrusted both to instinct alone.

And, in fact, we find that the more a cultivated reason deliberately devotes itself to the enjoyment of life and happiness, the more the man falls short of true contentment. From this fact there arises in many persons, if only they are candid enough to admit it, a certain degree of misology, hatred of reason. This is particularly the case with those who are most experienced in its use. After counting all the advantages which they draw — I will not say from the invention of the arts of common luxury — from the sciences (which in the end seem to them to be also a luxury of the understanding), they nevertheless find that they have actually brought more trouble on their shoulders instead of gaining in happiness; they 396 finally envy, rather than despise, the common run of men who are better guided by merely natural instinct and who do not permit their reason much influence on their conduct. And we must at least admit that a morose attitude or ingratitude to the goodness with which the world is governed is by no means found always among those who temper or refute the boasting eulogies which are given of the advantages of happiness and contentment with which reason is supposed to supply us. Rather, their judgment is based on the Idea of another and far more worthy purpose of their existence for which, instead of happiness, their reason is properly intended; this purpose, therefore, being the supreme condition to which the private purposes of men must, for the most part, defer.

Since reason is not competent to guide the will safely with regard to its objects and the satisfaction of all our needs (which it in part multiplies), to this end an innate instinct would have led with far more certainty. But reason is given to us as a practical faculty (i.e., one which is meant to have an influence on the will). As nature has elsewhere distributed capacities suitable to the functions they are to perform, reason's proper function must be to produce a will good in itself and not one good merely as a means, since for the former, reason is absolutely essential. This will need not be the sole and complete good, yet it must be the condition of all others, even of the desire for happiness. In this case it is entirely compatible with the wisdom of nature that the cultivation of reason, which is required for the former unconditional purpose, at least in this life restricts in many ways—indeed, can reduce to nothing—the achievement of the latter unconditional purpose, happiness. For one perceives that nature here does not proceed unsuitably to its purpose, because reason, which recognizes its highest practical vocation in the establishment of a good will, is capable of a contentment of its own kind (i.e., one that springs from the attainment of a purpose determined by reason), even though this injures the ends of inclination.

397   We have, then, to develop the concept of a will which is to be esteemed as good in itself without regard to anything else. It dwells already in the natural and sound understanding and does not need so much to be taught as only to be brought to

light. In the estimation of the total worth of our actions it always takes first place and is the condition of everything else. In order to show this, we shall take the concept of duty. It contains the concept of a good will, though with certain subjective restrictions and hindrances, but these are far from concealing it and making it unrecognizable, for they rather bring it out by contrast and make it shine forth all the more brightly.

I here omit all actions which are recognized as opposed to duty, even though they may be useful in one respect or another, for with these the question does not arise as to whether they may be done *from* duty, since they conflict with it. I also pass over actions which are really in accord with duty and to which one has no direct inclination, rather doing them because impelled to do so by another inclination. For it is easily decided whether an action in accord with duty is done from duty or for some selfish purpose. It is far more difficult to note this difference when the action is in accord with duty and, in addition, the subject has a direct inclination to do it. For example, it is in accord with duty that a dealer should not overcharge an inexperienced customer, and wherever there is much trade the prudent merchant does not do so, but has a fixed price for everyone so that a child may buy from him as cheaply as any other. Thus the customer is honestly served, but this is far from sufficient to warrant the belief that the merchant has behaved in this way from duty and principles of honesty. His own advantage required this behavior, but it cannot be assumed that over and above that he had a direct inclination to his customers and that, out of love, as it were, he gave none an advantage in price over another. The action was done neither from duty nor from direct inclination but only for a selfish purpose.

On the other hand, it is a duty to preserve one's life, and moreover everyone has a direct inclination to do so. But for that reason, the often anxious care which most men take of it has no intrinsic worth, and the maxim of doing so has no moral import. They preserve their lives according to duty, but 398 not from duty. But if adversities and hopeless sorrow completely take away the relish for life; if an unfortunate man, strong in soul, is indignant rather than despondent or dejected over his fate and wishes for death, and yet preserves his life without loving it and from neither inclination nor fear but from duty—then his maxim has moral merit.

To be kind where one can is a duty, and there are, moreover, many persons so sympathetically constituted that without any motive of vanity or selfishness they find an inner satisfaction in spreading joy and rejoice in the contentment of others which they have made possible. But I say that, however dutiful and however amiable it may be, that kind of action has no true moral worth. It is on a level with [actions done from] other inclinations, such as the inclination to honor, which, if fortunately directed to what in fact accords with duty and is generally useful and thus honorable, deserve praise and encouragement, but no esteem. For the maxim lacks the moral import of an action done not from inclination but from duty. But assume that the mind of that friend to mankind was clouded by a sorrow of his own which extinguished all sympathy with the lot of others, and though he still had the power to benefit others in distress their need left him untouched because he was preoccupied with his own. Now suppose him to tear himself, unsolicited by inclination, out of his dead insensibility and to do this action only from duty and without any inclination—then for the first time his action has genuine moral worth. Furthermore, if nature has put little sympathy into the heart of a man, and if he, though an honest man, is by temperament cold and indifferent to the sufferings of others perhaps because he is provided with special gifts of patience and fortitude and expects and even requires that others should have them too—and such a man would certainly not be the meanest product of nature—would not he find in himself a source from which to give himself a far higher worth than he could have got by having a good-natured temperament? This is unquestionably true even though nature did not make him philanthropic, for it is just here that the worth of character is brought out, which is morally the incomparably highest of all: he is beneficent not from inclination, but from duty.

To secure one's own happiness is at least indirectly a duty, for discontent with one's condition under pressure from many cares and amid unsatisfied wants could easily become a great temptation to transgress against duties. But, without any view to duty, all men have the strongest and deepest inclination to happiness, because in this Idea all inclinations are summed up. But the precept of happiness is often so formulated that it definitely thwarts some inclinations, and men can make no definite and certain concept of the sum of satisfaction of all inclinations, which goes under the name of happiness. It is not to be wondered at, therefore, that a single inclination, definite as to what it promises and as to the time at which it can be satisfied, can outweigh a fluctuating idea and that, for example, a man with the gout can choose to enjoy what he likes and to suffer what he may, because according to his calculations at least on this occasion he has not sacrificed the enjoyment of the present moment to a perhaps groundless expectation of a happiness supposed to lie in health. But even in this case if the universal inclination to happiness did not determine his will, and if health were not at least for him a necessary factor in these calculations, there would still remain, as in all other cases, a law that he ought to promote his happiness not from inclination but from duty. Only from this law could his conduct have true moral worth.

It is in this way, undoubtedly, that we should understand those passages of Scripture which command us to love our neighbor and even our enemy, for love as an inclination cannot be commanded. But beneficence from duty, even when no inclination impels it and even when it is opposed by a natural and unconquerable aversion, is practical love, not pathological[2] love; it resides in the will and not in the propensities of feeling, in principles of action and not in tender sympathy; and it alone can be commanded.

[Thus the first proposition of morality is that to have genu-

---

[2]Here as elsewhere Kant uses the word *pathological* to describe motives and actions arising from feeling or bodily impulses, with no suggestion of abnormality or disease.

ine moral worth, an action must be done from duty.] The second proposition is: An action done from duty does not have its moral worth in the purpose which is to be achieved through it but in the maxim whereby it is determined. Its moral value, therefore, does not depend upon the realization of the object of the action but merely on the principle of the volition by which the action is done irrespective of the objects of the faculty of desire. From the preceding discussion it is clear that the purposes we may have for our actions and their effects as ends and incentives of the will cannot give the actions any unconditional and moral worth. Wherein, then, can this worth lie, if it is not in the will in its relation to its hoped-for effect? It can lie nowhere else than in the principle of the will irrespective of the ends which can be realized by such action. For the will stands, as it were, at the crossroads halfway between its a priori principle which is formal and its posteriori incentive which is material. Since it must be determined by something, if it is done from duty it must be determined by the formal principle of volition as such, since every material principle has been withdrawn from it.

The third principle, as a consequence of the two preceding, I would express as follows: Duty is the necessity to do an action from respect for law. I can certainly have an inclination to an object as an effect of the proposed action, but I can never have respect for it precisely because it is a mere effect and not an activity of a will. Similarly, I can have no respect for any inclination whatsoever, whether my own or that of another; in the former case I can at most approve of it and in the latter I can even love it (i.e., see it as favorable to my own advantage). But that which is connected with my will merely as ground and not as consequence, that which does not serve my inclination but overpowers it or at least excludes it from being considered in making a choice — in a word, law itself — can be an object of respect and thus a command. Now as an act from duty wholly excludes the influence of inclination and therewith every object of the will, nothing remains which can determine the will objectively except law and subjectively except pure respect for this practical law. This subjec-

tive element is the maxim* that I should follow such a law
even if it thwarts all my inclinations.

Thus the moral worth of an action does not lie in the effect
which is expected from it or in any principle of action which
has to borrow its motive from this expected effect. For all
these effects (agreeableness of my own condition, indeed
even the promotion of the happiness of others) could be
brought about through other causes and would not require
the will of a rational being, while the highest and unconditional good can be found only in such a will. Therefore the
preeminent good can consist only in the conception of law in
itself (which can be present only in a rational being) so far as
this conception and not the hoped-for effect is the determining ground of the will. This preeminent good, which we call
moral, is already present in the person who acts according to
this conception, and we do not have to look for it first in the
result.†

---

*A maxim is the subjective principle of volition. The objective princi-
ple (i.e., that which would serve all rational beings also subjectively as a
practical principle if reason had full power over the faculty of desire) is
the practical law.

† It might be objected that I seek to take refuge in an obscure feeling
behind the word "respect," instead of clearly resolving the question
with a concept of reason. But though respect is a feeling, it is not one
received through any [outer] influence but is self-wrought by a rational
concept; thus it differs specifically from all feelings of the former kind
which may be referred to inclination or fear. What I recognize directly as
a law for myself I recognize with respect, which means merely the
consciousness of the submission of my will to a law without the inter-
vention of other influences on my mind. The direct determination of the
will by law and the consciousness of this determination is respect; thus
respect can be regarded as the effect of the law on the subject and not as
the cause of the law. Respect is properly the conception of a worth
which thwarts my self-love. Thus it is regarded as an object neither of
inclination nor of fear, though it has something analogous to both. The
only object of respect is law, and indeed only the law which we impose
on ourselves and yet recognize as necessary in itself. As a law we are

(Footnote continued on next page)

402   But what kind of law can that be, the conception of which must determine the will without reference to the expected result? Under this condition alone can the will be called absolutely good without qualification. Since I have robbed the will of all impulses which could come to it from obedience to any law, nothing remains to serve as a principle of the will except universal conformity to law as such. That is, I ought never to act in such a way that I could not also will that my maxim should be a universal law. Strict conformity to law as such (without assuming any particular law applicable to certain actions) serves as the principle of the will, and it must serve as such a principle if duty is not to be a vain delusion and chimerical concept. The common sense of mankind (*gemeine Menschenvernunft*) in its practical judgments is in perfect agreement with this and has this principle constantly in view.

Let the question, for example, be: May I, when in distress, make a promise with the intention not to keep it? I easily distinguish the two meanings which the question can have, viz., whether it is prudent to make a false promise, or whether it conforms to duty. The former can undoubtedly be often the case, though I do see clearly that it is not sufficient merely to escape from the present difficulty by this expedient, but that I must consider whether inconveniences much greater than the present one may not later spring from this lie. Even with all my supposed cunning, the consequences cannot be so easily foreseen. Loss of credit might be far more disadvantageous than the misfortune I am now seeking to avoid, and it is hard

---

subject to it without consulting self-love; as imposed on us by ourselves, it is a consequence of our will. In the former respect it is analogous to fear and in the latter to inclination. All respect for a person is only respect for the law (of righteousness, etc.) of which the person provides an example. Because we see the improvement of our talents as a duty, we think of a person of talent as the example of a law, as it were (the law that we should by practice become like him in his talents), and that constitutes our respect. All so-called moral interest consists solely in respect for the law.

to tell whether it might not be more prudent to act according to a universal maxim and to make it a habit not to promise anything without intending to fulfill it. But it is soon clear to me that such a maxim is based only on an apprehensive concern with consequences.

To be truthful from duty, however, is an entirely different thing from being truthful out of fear of untoward consequences, for in the former case the concept of the action itself contains a law for me, while in the latter I must first look about to see what results for me may be connected with it. To deviate from the principle of duty is certainly bad, but to be unfaithful to my maxim of prudence can sometimes be very advantageous to me, though it is certainly safer to abide by it. The shortest but most infallible way to find the answer to the question as to whether a deceitful promise is consistent with duty is to ask myself: Would I be content that my maxim of extricating myself from difficulty by a false promise should hold as a universal law for myself as well as for others? And could I say to myself that everyone may make a false promise when he is in a difficulty from which he otherwise cannot escape? Immediately I see that I could will the lie but not a universal law to lie. For with such a law there would be no promises at all, inasmuch as it would be futile to make a pretense of my intention in regard to future actions to those who would not believe this pretense or—if they overhastily did so—would pay me back in my own coin. Thus my maxim would necessarily destroy itself as soon as it was made a universal law.

I do not, therefore, need any penetrating acuteness to discern what I have to do in order that my volition may be morally good. Inexperienced in the course of the world, incapable of being prepared for all its contingencies, I only ask myself: Can I will that my maxim become a universal law? If not, it must be rejected, not because of any disadvantage accruing to myself or even to others, but because it cannot enter as a principle into a possible enactment of universal law, and reason extorts from me an immediate respect for such legislation. I do not as yet discern on what it is grounded (this is a question the philosopher may investigate), but I at least understand that it is an estimation of a worth which far outweighs all the worth of whatever is recommended by the inclinations, and that the necessity that I act from pure respect for the practical law constitutes my duty. To duty every other motive must give place, because duty is the condition of a will good in itself, whose worth transcends everything.

Thus within the moral knowledge of ordinary human reason (*gemeine Menschenvernunft*) we have attained its principle. To be sure, ordinary human reason does not think this principle abstractly in such a universal form, but it always has the principle in view and uses it as the standard for its judgments. It would be easy to show how ordinary human reason, with this compass, knows well how to distinguish what is good, what is bad, and what is consistent or inconsistent with duty. Without in the least teaching common reason anything new, we need only to draw its attention to its own principle (in the manner of Socrates), thus showing that neither science nor philosophy is needed in order to know what one has to do in order to be honest and good, and even wise and virtuous. We might have conjectured beforehand that the knowledge of what everyone is obliged to do and thus also to know would be within the reach of everyone, even of the most ordinary man. Here we cannot but admire the great advantages which the practical faculty of judgment has over the theoretical in ordinary human understanding. In the theoretical, if ordinary reason ventures to go beyond the laws of experience and perceptions of the senses, it falls into sheer inconceivabilities and self-contradictions, or at least into a chaos of uncertainty, obscurity, and instability. In the practical, on the other hand, the power of judgment first shows itself to advantage when common understanding excludes all sensuous incentives from practical laws. It then even becomes subtle, quibbling with its own conscience or with other claims to what should be called right, or wishing to determine accurately, for its own instruction, the worth of certain actions. But the most remarkable thing about ordinary human understanding in its practical concern is that it may have as much hope as any philosopher of hitting the mark. In fact, it is almost more certain to do so that the philosopher, for

404

while he has no principle which common understanding lacks, his judgment is easily confused by a mass of irrelevant considerations so that it easily turns aside from the correct way. Would it not, therefore, be wiser in moral matters to acquiesce in ordinary reasonable judgment and at most to call in philosophy in order to make the system of morals more complete and comprehensible and its rules more convenient for use (especially in disputation), than to steer the ordinary understanding from its happy simplicity in practical matters and to lead it through philosophy into a new path of inquiry and instruction?

Innocence is indeed a glorious thing, but it is very sad that it cannot well maintain itself, being easily led astray. For this reason, even wisdom—which consists more in acting than in knowing—needs science, not so as to learn from it but to secure admission and permanence to its precepts. Man feels in himself a powerful counterpoise against all commands of duty which reason presents to him as so deserving of respect. This counterpoise is his needs and inclinations, the complete satisfaction of which he sums up under the name of happiness. Now reason issues inexorable commands without promising anything to the inclinations. It disregards, as it were, and holds in contempt those claims which are so impetuous and yet so plausible, and which refuse to be suppressed by any command. From this a natural dialectic arises, i.e., a propensity to argue against the stern laws of duty and their validity, or at least to place their purity and strictness in doubt and, where possible, to make them more accordant with our wishes and inclinations. This is equivalent to corrupting them in their very foundations and destroying their dignity—a thing which even ordinary practical reason cannot finally call good.

In this way ordinary human reason is impelled to go outside its sphere and to take a step into the field of practical philosophy. But it is forced to do so not by any speculative need, which never occurs to it so long as it is satisfied to remain merely healthy reason; rather, it is impelled on practical grounds to obtain information and clear instruction respecting the source of its principle and the correct definition of this principle in its opposition to the maxims based on need and inclination. It seeks this information in order to escape from the perplexity of opposing claims and to avoid the danger of losing all genuine moral principles through the equivocation in which it is easily involved. Thus when ordinary practical reason cultivates itself, a dialectic surreptitiously ensues which forces it to seek aid in philosophy, just as the same thing happens in the theoretical use of reason. Ordinary practical reason, like theoretical reason, will find rest only in a complete critical examination of our reason.

Second Section
Transition from Popular Moral Philosophy to the Metaphysics of Morals

406   Although we have derived our earlier concept of duty from the ordinary use of our practical reason, it is by no means to be inferred that we have treated it as an empirical concept. On the contrary, if we attend to our experience of the way men act, we meet frequent and, as we must confess, justified complaints that we cannot cite a single sure example of the disposition to act from pure duty. There are also justified complaints that, though much may be done that accords with what duty commands, it is nevertheless always doubtful whether it is done from duty and thus whether it has moral worth. There have always been philosophers who for this reason have absolutely denied the reality of this disposition in human actions, attributing everything to more or less refined self-love. They have done so without questioning the correctness of the concept of morality. Rather they spoke with sincere regret of the frailty and corruption of human nature, which is noble enough to take as its precept an Idea so worthy of respect but which at the same time is too weak to follow it, employing reason, which should give laws for human nature, only to provide for the interest of the inclinations either singly or, at best, in their greatest possible harmony with one another.

It is, in fact, absolutely impossible by experience to discern   407
with complete certainty a single case in which the maxim of
an action, however much it might conform to duty, rested
solely on moral grounds and on the conception of one's duty.
It sometimes happens that in the most searching self-exami-
nation we can find nothing except the moral ground of duty
which could have been powerful enough to move us to this or
that good action and to such great sacrifice. But from this we
cannot by any means conclude with certainty that a secret
impulse of self-love, falsely appearing as the Idea of duty, was
not actually the true determining cause of the will. For we
like to flatter ourselves with a pretended nobler motive, while
in fact even the strictest examination can never lead us entirely behind the secret incentives, for when moral worth is in
question it is not a matter of actions which one sees but of
their inner principles which one does not see.

Moreover, one cannot better serve the wishes of those who
ridicule all morality as a mere phantom of human imagination
overreaching itself through self-conceit than by conceding
that the concepts of duty must be derived only from experience (for they are ready, from indolence, to believe that this
is true of all other concepts too). For, by this concession, a
sure triumph is prepared for them. Out of love for humanity I
am willing to admit that most of our actions are in accord with
duty; but if we look more closely at our thoughts and aspira-
tions, we come everywhere upon the dear self, which is
always turning up, and it is this instead of the stern command
of duty (which would often require self-denial) which supports our plans. One need not be an enemy of virtue, but only
a cool observer who does not confuse even the liveliest aspi-
ration for the good with its actuality, to be sometimes doubtful whether true virtue can really be found anywhere in the
world. This is especially true as one's years increase and the
power of judgment is made wiser by experience and more
acute in observation. This being so, nothing can secure us
against the complete abandonment of our ideas of duty and
preserve in us a well-founded respect for its law except the
conviction that, even if there never were actions springing

408 from such pure sources, our concern is not whether this or that was done, but that reason of itself and independently of all appearances commanded what ought to be done. Our concern is with actions of which perhaps the world has never had an example, with actions whose feasibility might be seriously doubted by those who base everything on experience, and yet with actions inexorably commanded by reason. For example, pure sincerity in friendship can be demanded of every man, and this demand is not in the least diminished if a sincere friend has never existed, because this duty, as duty in general, prior to all experience lies in the Idea of reason which determines the will on a priori grounds.

No experience, it is clear, can give occasion for inferring the possibility of such apodictic laws. This is especially clear when we add that, unless we wish to deny all truth to the concept of morality and renounce its application to any possible object, we cannot refuse to admit that the law is of such broad significance that it holds not merely for men but for all rational beings as such; we must grant that it must be valid with absolute necessity, and not merely under contingent conditions and with exceptions. For with what right could we bring into unlimited respect something that might be valid only under contingent human conditions? And how could laws of the determination of our will be held to be laws of the determination of the will of any rational being whatever and of ourselves in so far as we are rational beings, if they were merely empirical and did not have their origin completely a priori in pure, but practical, reason?

Nor could one given poorer counsel to morality than to attempt to derive it from examples. For each example of morality which is exhibited must itself have been previously judged according to principles of morality to see whether it was worthy to serve as an original example or model. By no means could it authoritatively furnish the concept of morality. Even the Holy One of the Gospel must be compared with our ideal of moral perfection before He is recognized as such; even He says of Himself, "Why call ye Me (Whom you see) good? None is good (the archetype of the good) except God

only (Whom you do not see)." But whence do we have the   40:
concept of God as the highest good? Solely from the Idea of
moral perfection which reason formulates a priori and which
it inseparably connects with the concept of a free will. Imita-
tion has no place in moral matters, and examples serve only
for encouragement. That is, they put beyond question the
possibility of performing what the law commands, and they
make visible that which the practical rule expresses more
generally. But they can never justify our guiding ourselves by
examples and our setting aside their true original, which lies
in reason.

If there is thus no genuine supreme principle of morality
which does not rest on pure reason alone independent of all
possible experience, I do not believe it is necessary even to
ask whether it is well to exhibit these concepts generally (*in
abstracto*), which, together with the principles belonging to
them, are established a priori. At any rate, the question need
not be asked if knowledge of them is to be distinguished from
ordinary knowledge and called philosophical. But in our
times this question may be necessary. For if we collected
votes as to whether pure rational knowledge separated from
all experience (i.e., a metaphysics of morals) or popular practical philosophy is to be preferred, it is easily guessed on
which side the majority would stand.

This condescension to popular notions is certainly very
commendable once the ascent to the principles of pure reason has been satisfactorily accomplished. That would mean
the prior establishment of the doctrine of morals on metaphysics and then, when it is established, procuring a hearing
for it through popularization. But it is extremely absurd to
want to achieve popular appeal in the first investigation,
where everything depends on the correctness of the fundamental principles. Not only can this procedure never make
claim to that rarest merit of true philosophical popularity,
since there is really no art in being generally comprehensible
if one thereby renounces all basic insight; but it produces a
disgusting jumble of patched-up observations and half-rea-
soned principles. Shallow pates enjoy this, for it is very useful

everyday chitchat, while the more sensible feel confused
and dissatisfied and avert their eyes without being able to
help themselves. But philosophers, who see through this delusion, get little hearing when they call people away from this
410   would-be popularity so that they may have genuine popular
appeal once they have gained a definite understanding.

One need only look at the essays on morality favored by
popular taste. One will sometimes meet with the particular
vocation of human nature (but occasionally with the Idea of a
rational nature in general), sometimes perfection and sometimes happiness, here moral feeling, there fear of God, a little
of this and a little of that in a marvelous mixture. It never
occurs to the authors, however, to ask whether the principles
of morality are, after all, to be sought anywhere in knowledge
of human nature (which we can derive only from experience). And if this is not the case, if the principles are a priori,
free from everything empirical, and found exclusively in pure
rational concepts and not at all in any other place, they never
ask whether they should undertake this investigation as a
separate inquiry (i.e., as pure practical philosophy) or (if one
may use a name so decried) a metaphysics* of morals. They
never think of dealing with it alone and bringing it by itself to
completeness and of requiring the public, which desires popularization, to await the outcome of this undertaking.

But a completely isolated metaphysics of morals, mixed
with no anthropology, no theology, no physics or hyperphys-
ics, and even less with occult qualities (which might be called
hypophysical), is not only an indispensable substrate of all
theoretically sound and definite knowledge of duties; it is

---

*If one wishes, the pure philosophy (metaphysics) of morals can be
distinguished from the applied (i.e., applied to human nature), just as
pure mathematics and pure logic are distinguished from applied mathematics and applied logic. By this designation one is immediately re-
minded that moral principles are not founded on the peculiarities of
human nature but must stand of themselves a priori, and that from such
principles practical rules for every rational nature, and accordingly for
man, must be derivable.

also a desideratum of the highest importance to the actual fulfillment of its precepts. For the thought of duty and of the moral law generally, with no admixture of empirical inducements, has an influence on the human heart so much more powerful than all other incentives* which may be derived from the empirical field that reason, in the consciousness of its dignity, despises them and gradually becomes master over them. It has this influence only through reason alone, which thereby first realizes that it can of itself be practical. A mixed theory of morals which is put together from incentives of feelings and inclinations and from rational concepts must, on the other hand, make the mind vacillate between motives which cannot be brought together under any principle and which can lead only accidentally to the good, and frequently lead to the bad.

From what has been said it is clear that all moral concepts have their seat and origin entirely a priori in reason. This is just as much the case in the most ordinary reason as in the reason which is speculative to the highest degree. It is obvious that they can be abstracted from no empirical and hence merely contingent cognitions. In the purity of origin lies their worthiness to serve us as supreme practical principles, and to the extent that something empirical is added to them, just this

411

---

*I have a letter from the late excellent Sulzer in which he asks me why the theories of virtue accomplish so little even though they contain so much that is convincing to reason. My answer was delayed in order that I might make it complete. The answer is only that the teachers themselves have not completely clarified their concepts, and when they wish to make up for this by hunting in every quarter for motives to the morally good so as to make their physic right strong, they spoil it. For the commonest observation shows that if we imagine an act of honesty performed with a steadfast soul and sundered from all view to any advantage in this or another world and even under the greatest temptations of need or allurement, it far surpasses and eclipses any similar action which was affected in the least by any foreign incentive; it elevates the soul and arouses the wish to be able to act in this way. Even moderately young children feel this impression, and one should never represent duties to them in any other way.

much is subtracted from their genuine influence and from the unqualified worth of actions. Furthermore, it is evident that it is not only of the greatest necessity from a theoretical point of view when it is a question of speculation but also of the utmost practical importance to derive the concepts and laws of morals from pure reason and to present them pure and unmixed, and to determine the scope of this entire practical but pure rational knowledge (the entire faculty of pure practical reason) without making the principles depend upon the particular nature of human reason, as speculative philosophy 412 may permit and even find necessary. But since moral laws should hold for every rational being as such, the principles must be derived from the universal concept of a rational being in general. In this manner all morals, which need anthropology for their application to men, must be completely developed first as pure philosophy (i.e., metaphysics), independently of anthropology (a thing feasibly done in such distinct fields of knowledge). For we know well that if we are not in possession of such a metaphysics, it is not merely futile [to try to] define accurately for the purposes of speculative judgment the moral element of duty in all actions which accord with duty, but impossible to base morals on legitimate principles for even ordinary practical use, especially in moral instruction; and it is only in this manner that pure moral dispositions can be produced and engrafted on men's minds for the purpose of the highest good in the world.

In this study we do not advance merely from the common moral judgment (which here is very worthy of respect) to the philosophical, as this has already been done; but we advance by natural stages from popular philosophy (which goes no farther than it can grope by means of examples) to metaphysics (which is not held back by anything empirical and which, as it must measure out the entire scope of rational knowledge of this kind, reaches even Ideas, where examples fail us). In order to make this advance, we must follow and clearly present the practical faculty of reason from its universal rules of determination to the point where the concept of duty arises from it.

Everything in nature works according to laws. Only a rational being has the capacity of acting according to the *conception* of laws (i.e., according to principles). This capacity is the will. Since reason is required for the derivation of actions from laws, will is nothing less than practical reason. If reason infallibly determines the will, the actions which such a being recognizes as objectively necessary are also subjectively necessary. That is, the will is a faculty of choosing only that which reason, independently of inclination, recognizes as practically necessary (i.e., as good). But if reason of itself does not sufficiently determine the will, and if the will is subjugated to subjective conditions (certain incentives)   413 which do not always agree with the objective conditions — in a word, if the will is not of itself in complete accord with reason (which is the actual case with men), then the actions which are recognized as objectively necessary are subjectively contingent, and the determination of such a will according to objective laws is a constraint. That is, the relation of objective laws to a will which is not completely good is conceived as the determination of the will of a rational being by principles of reason to which this will is not by its nature necessarily obedient.

The conception of an objective principle, so far as it constrains a will, is a command (of reason), and the formula of this command is called an *imperative*.

All imperatives are expressed by an "ought" and thereby indicate the relation of an objective law of reason to a will which is not in its subjective constitution necessarily determined by this law. This relation is that of constraint. Imperatives say that it would be good to do or to refrain from doing something, but they say it to a will which does not always do something simply because the thing is presented to it as good to do. Practical good is what determines the will by means of the conception of reason and hence not by subjective causes but objectively, on grounds which are valid for every rational being as such. It is distinguished from the pleasant, as that which has an influence on the will only by means of a sensation from purely subjective causes, which hold for the senses only of this or that person and not as a principle of reason which holds for everyone.*

414   A perfectly good will, therefore, would be equally subject to objective laws of the good, but it could not be conceived as constrained by them to accord with them, because it can be determined to act by its own subjective constitution only through the conception of the good. Thus no imperatives hold for the divine will or, more generally, for a holy will. The "ought" here is out of place, for the volition of itself is necessarily in unison with the law. Therefore imperatives are only formulas expressing the relation of objective laws of volition in general to the subjective imperfection of the will of this or that rational being, for example, the human will.

All imperatives command either *hypothetically* or *categorically*. The former present the practical necessity of a possible action as a means to achieving something else which one desires (or which one may possibly desire). The categorical imperative would be one which presented an action as of itself objectively necessary, without regard to any other end.

Since every practical law presents a possible action as good and thus as necessary for a subject practically determinable by

413   *The dependence of the faculty of desire on sensations is called inclination, and inclination always indicates a need. The dependence of a contingently determinable will on principles of reason, however, is called interest. An interest is present only in a dependent will which is not of itself always in accord with reason; in the divine will we cannot conceive of an interest. But even the human will can take an interest in something without thereby acting from interest. The former means the practical interest in the action; the latter, the pathological interest in the object of the action. The former indicates only the dependence of the will on principles of reason in themselves, while the latter indicates dependence on the principles of reason for the purpose of inclination, since reason gives only the practical rule by which the needs of inclination are to be aided. In the former case the action interests me, and in the latter the object of the action (so far as it is pleasant for me) interests me. In the First Section we have seen that, in the case of an action done from duty, no regard must be given to the interest in the object, but merely to the action itself and its principle in reason (i.e., the law).

reason, all imperatives are formulas of the determination of action which is necessary by the principle of a will which is in any way good. If the action is good only as a means to something else, the imperative is hypothetical; but if it is thought of as good in itself, and hence as necessary in a will which of itself conforms to reason as the principle of this will, the imperative is categorical.

The imperative thus says what action possible for me would be good, and it presents the practical rule in relation to a will which does not forthwith perform an action simply because it is good, in part because the subject does not always know that the action is good, and in part (when he does know it) because his maxims can still be opposed to the objective principles of a practical reason.

The hypothetical imperative, therefore, says only that the action is good to some purpose, possible or actual. In the former case, it is a problematical, in the latter an assertorical, practical principle. The categorical imperative, which declares the action to be of itself objectively necessary without making any reference to any end in view (i.e., without having any other purpose), holds as an apodictical practical principle. 415

We can think of what is possible only through the powers of some rational being as a possible end in view of any will. As a consequence, the principles of action thought of as necessary to attain a possible end in view which can be achieved by them, are in reality infinitely numerous. All sciences have some practical part consisting of problems which presuppose some purpose as well as imperatives directing how it can be reached. These imperatives can therefore be called, generally, imperatives of skill. Whether the purpose is reasonable and good is not in question at all, for the questions concerns only what must be done in order to attain it. The precepts to be followed by a physician in order to cure his patient and by a poisoner to bring about certain death are of equal value in so far as each does that which will perfectly accomplish his purpose. Since in early youth we do not know what purposes we may have in the course of our life, parents seek to let their children learn a great many things and provide for skill in the use of means to all sorts of ends which they might choose, among which they cannot determine whether any one of them will become their child's actual purpose, though it may be that someday he may have it as his actual purpose. And this anxiety is so great that they commonly neglect to form and correct their children's judgment on the worth of the things which they may make their ends.

There is one end, however, which we may presuppose as actual in all rational beings so far as imperatives apply to them, that is, so far as they are dependent beings. There is one purpose which they not only *can* have but which we can presuppose that they all *do* have by a necessity of nature. This purpose is happiness. The hypothetical imperative which represents the practical necessity of an action as means to the promotion of happiness is an assertorical imperative. We may not expound it as necessary to a merely uncertain and merely possible purpose, but as necessary to a purpose which we can 416 a priori and with assurance assume for everyone because it belongs to his essence. Skill in the choice of means to one's own highest well-being can be called prudence* in the narrowest sense. Thus the imperative which refers to the choice of means to one's own happiness (i.e., the precept of prudence) is still only hypothetical, and the action is not commanded absolutely but commanded only as a means to another end in view.

Finally, there is one imperative which directly commands certain conduct without making its condition some purpose to be reached by it. This imperative is categorical. It concerns not the ·material of the action and its intended result, but the

---

*The word "prudence" may be taken in two senses, and it may bear the names of prudence with reference to things of the world and private prudence. The former sense means the skill of a man in having an influence on others so as to use them for his own purposes. The latter is the ability to unite all these purposes to his own lasting advantage. The worth of the first is finally reduced to the latter, and of one who is prudent in the former sense but not in the latter we might better say that he is clever and cunning yet, on the whole, imprudent.

form and principle from which it originates. What is essentially good in it consists in the mental disposition, the result being what it may. This imperative may be called the imperative of morality.

Volition according to these three principles is plainly distinguished by the dissimilarity in the constraints by which they subject the will. In order to clarify this dissimilarity, I believe that they are most suitably named if one says that they are either rules of skill, counsels of prudence, or commands (laws) of morality, respectively. For law alone implies the concept of an unconditional and objective and hence universally valid necessity, and commands are laws which must be obeyed even against inclination. Counsels do indeed involve necessity, but a necessity that can hold only under a subjectively contingent condition (i.e., whether this or that man counts this or that as part of his happiness). The categorical imperative, on the other hand, is restricted by no condition. As absolutely, though practically, necessary it can be called a command in the strict sense. We could also call the first imperatives *technical* (belonging to art), the second *pragmatic** (belonging to well-being), and the third *moral* (belonging to free conduct as such, i.e., to morals). 417

The question now arises: How are all these imperatives possible? This question does not require an answer as to how the action which the imperative commands can be performed, but only an answer as to how the constraint of the will, which the imperative expresses in setting the problem, can be conceived. How an imperative of skill is possible requires no particular discussion. Whoever wills the end, so far as reason has decisive influence on his action, wills also the indispensably necessary steps to it that he can take. This

---

*It seems to me that the proper meaning of the word "pragmatic" could be most accurately defined in this way. For sanctions which properly flow not from the law of states as necessary statutes but from provision for the general welfare are called pragmatic. A history is pragmatically composed when it teaches prudence (i.e., instructs the world how it could provide for its interest better than, or at least as well as, has been done in the past).

proposition, in what concerns the will, is analytical; for, in the willing of an object as an effect, my causality, as an acting cause of this effect shown in my use of the means to it, is already thought, and the imperative derives the concept of actions necessary to this purpose from the concept of willing this purpose. Synthetical propositions undoubtedly are necessary for determining the means to a proposed end, but they do not concern the ground, the act of the will, but only the way to achieve the object. Mathematics teaches, by synthetical propositions only, that in order to bisect a line according to an infallible principle, I must make two intersecting arcs from each of its extremities; but if I know the proposed result can be obtained only by such an action, then it is an analytical proposition that, if I fully will the effect, I must also will the action necessary to produce it. For it is one and the same thing to conceive of something as an effect which is in a certain way possible through me, and to conceive of myself as acting in this way.

If it were only easy to give a definite concept of happiness, the imperatives of prudence would perfectly correspond to those of skill and would likewise be analytical. For it could then be said in this case as well as in the former that whoever wills the end wills also (necessarily according to reason) the only means to it which are in his power. But it is a misfortune that the concept of happiness is so indefinite that, although each person wishes to attain it, he can never definitely and self-consistently state what it is that he really wishes and wills. The reason for this is that all elements which belong to the concept of happiness are empirical (i.e, they must be taken from experience), while for the Idea of happiness an absolute whole, a maximum, of well-being is needed in my present and in every future condition. Now it is impossible for even a most clear-sighted and most capable but finite being to form here a definite concept of that which he really wills. If he wills riches, how much anxiety, envy, and intrigues might he not thereby draw upon his shoulders! If he wills much knowledge and vision, perhaps it might become only an eye that much sharper to show him as more dreadful the evils which are now hidden from him and which are yet unavoidable; or it might be to burden his desires—which already sufficiently engage him—with even more needs! If he wills long life, who guarantees that it will not be long misery! If he wills at least health, how often has not the discomfort of his body restrained him from excesses into which perfect health would have led him? In short, he is not capable, on any principle and with complete certainty, of ascertaining what would make him truly happy; omniscience would be needed for this. He cannot, therefore, act according to definite principles so as to be happy, but only according to empirical counsels (e.g., those of diet, economy, courtesy, restraint, etc.) which are shown by experience best to promote well-being on the average. Hence the imperatives of prudence cannot, in the strict sense, command (i.e., present actions objectively as practically necessary); thus they are to be taken as counsels (*consilia*) rather than as commands (*praecepta*) of reason, and the task of determining infallibly and universally what action will promote the happiness of a rational being is completely unsolvable. There can be no imperative which would, in the strict sense, command us to do what makes for happiness, because happiness is an ideal not of reason but of imagination, depending only on empirical grounds which one would expect in vain to determine an action through which the totality of consequences—which in fact is infinite—could be achieved. Assuming that the means to happiness could be infallibly stated, this imperative of prudence would be an analytically practical proposition for it differs from the imperative of skill only in that its purpose is given, while in the imperative of skill it is merely a possible purpose. Since both, however, command the means to that which one presupposes as a willed purpose, the imperative which commands the willing of the means to him who wills the end is in both cases analytical. There is, consequently, no difficulty in seeing the possibility of such an imperative.

    To see how the imperative of morality is possible, then, is without doubt the only question needing an answer. It is not hypothetical, and thus the objectively conceived necessity cannot be supported by any presupposed purpose, as was the case with the hypothetical imperatives. But it must not be overlooked that it cannot be shown by any example (i.e., it cannot be empirically shown) that there is such an imperative. Rather, it is to be suspected that all imperatives which appear to be categorical are tacitly hypothetical. For instance, when it is said, "Thou shalt not make a false promise," we assume that the necessity of this prohibition is not a mere counsel for the sake of escaping some other evil, so that it would read: "Thou shalt not make a false promise, lest, if it comes to light, thou ruinest thy credit." [In so doing] we assume that an action of this kind must be regarded as in itself bad and that the imperative prohibiting it is categorical, but we cannot show with certainty by any example that the will is here determined by the law alone without any other incentives, although it appears to be so. For it is always possible that secretly fear of disgrace, and perhaps also obscure apprehension of other dangers, may have had an influence on the will. Who can prove by experience the nonexistence of a cause when experience shows us only that we do not perceive the cause? In such a case the so-called moral imperative, which as such appears to be categorical and unconditional, would be actually only a pragmatic precept which makes us attentive to our own advantage and teaches us to consider it.

420   Thus we shall have to investigate purely a priori the possibility of a categorical imperative, for we do not have the advantage that experience would show us the reality of this imperative so that the [demonstration of its] possibility would be necessary only for its explanation, and not for its establishment. In the meantime, this much at least may be seen: the categorical imperative alone can be taken as a practical *law*, while all other imperatives may be called principles of the will but not laws. This is because what is necessary merely for the attainment of some chosen end can be regarded as itself contingent and we get rid of the precept once we give up the end in view, whereas the unconditional command leaves the will no freedom to choose the opposite. Thus it alone implies the necessity which we require of a law.

Secondly, in the case of the categorical imperative or law of morality, the cause of the difficulty in discerning its possibility is very weighty. This imperative is an a priori synthetical practical proposition* and since to discern the possibility of propositions of this sort is so difficult in theoretical knowledge it may well be gathered that it will be no less difficult in practical knowledge.

In attacking this problem, we will first inquire whether the mere concept of a categorical imperative does not also furnish the formula containing the proposition which alone can be a categorical imperative. For even when we know the formula of the imperative, to learn how such an absolute command is possible will require difficult and special labors which we shall postpone to the last Section.

If I think of a hypothetical imperative as such, I do not know what it will contain until the condition is stated [under which it is an imperative]. But if I think of a categorical imperative, I know immediately what it will contain. For since the imperative contains, besides the law, only the necessity of the maxim† of acting in accordance with the law, while the law contains no condition to which it is restricted, nothing remains except the universality of law as such to   421

---

*I connect a priori, and hence necessarily, the action with the will without supposing as a condition that there is any inclination [to the action] (though I do so only objectively, i.e., under the Idea of a reason which would have complete power over all subjective motives). This is, therefore, a practical proposition which does not analytically derive the willing of an action from some other volition already presupposed (for we do not have such a perfect will); it rather connects it directly with the concept of the will of a rational being as something which is not contained within it.

†A maxim is the subjective principle of acting and must be distinguished from the objective principle (i.e., the practical law). The former contains the practical rule which reason determines according to the conditions of the subject (often his ignorance or inclinations) and is thus the principle according to which the subject acts. The law, on the other hand, is the objective principle valid for every rational being, and the principle by which it ought to act, i.e., an imperative.

which the maxim of the action should conform; and this conformity alone is what is represented as necessary by the imperative.

There is, therefore, only one categorical imperative. It is: Act only according to that maxim by which you can at the same time will that it should become a universal law.

Now if all imperatives of duty can be derived from this one imperative as a principle, we can at least show what we understand by the concept of duty and what it means, even though it remain undecided whether that which is called duty is an empty concept or not.

The universality of law according to which effects are produced constitutes what is properly called nature in the most general sense (as to form) (i.e., the existence of things so far as it is determined by universal laws). [By analogy], then, the universal imperative of duty can be expressed as follows: Act as though the maxim of your action were by your will to become a universal law of nature.

We shall now enumerate some duties, adopting the usual division of them into duties to ourselves and to others and into perfect and imperfect duties.*

422   1. A man who is reduced to despair by a series of evils feels a weariness with life but is still in possession of his reason sufficiently to ask whether it would not be contrary to his duty to himself to take his own life. Now he asks whether the maxim of his action could become a universal law of nature. His maxim, however is: For love of myself, I make it my principle to shorten my life when by a longer duration it threatens more evil than satisfaction. But it is questionable

---

*It must be noted here that I reserve the division of duties for a future *Metaphysics of Morals* and that the division here stands as only an arbitrary one (chosen in order to arrange my examples). For the rest, by a perfect duty I here understand a duty which permits no exception in the interest of inclination; thus I have not merely outer but also inner perfect duties. This runs contrary to the usage adopted in the schools, but I am not disposed to defend it here because it is all one to my purpose whether this is conceded or not.

whether this principle of self-love could become a universal law of nature. One immediately sees a contradiction in a system of nature whose law would be to destroy life by the feeling whose special office is to impel the improvement of life. In this case it would not exist as nature; hence that maxim cannot obtain as a law of nature, and thus it wholly contradicts the supreme principle of all duty.

2. Another man finds himself forced by need to borrow money. He well knows that he will not be able to repay it, but he also sees that nothing will be lent him if he does not firmly promise to repay it at a certain time. He desires to make such a promise, but he has enough conscience to ask himself whether it is not improper and opposed to duty to relieve his distress in such a way. Now, assuming he does decide to do so, the maxim of his action would be as follows: When I believe myself to be in need of money, I will borrow money and promise to repay it, although I know I shall never be able to do so. Now this principle of self-love or of his own benefit may very well be compatible with his whole future welfare, but the question is whether it is right. He changes the pretension of self-love into a universal law and then puts the question: How would it be if my maxim became a universal law? He immediately sees that it could never hold as a universal law of nature and be consistent with itself; rather it must necessarily contradict itself. For the universality of a law which says that anyone who believes himself to be in need could promise what he pleased with the intention of not fulfilling it would make the promise itself and the end to be accomplished by it impossible; no one would believe what was promised to him but would only laugh at any such assertion as vain pretense.

3. A third finds in himself a talent which could, by means of   423
some cultivation, make him in many respects a useful man. But he finds himself in comfortable circumstances and prefers indulgence in pleasure to troubling himself with broadening and improving his fortunate natural gifts. Now, however, let him ask whether his maxim of neglecting his gifts, besides agreeing with his propensity to idle amusement,

agrees also with what is called duty. He sees that a system of nature could indeed exist in accordance with such a law, even though man (like the inhabitants of the South Sea Islands) should let his talents rust and resolve to devote his life merely to idleness, indulgence, and propagation—in a word, to pleasure. But he cannot possibly will that this should become a universal law of nature or that it should be implanted in us by a natural instinct. For, as a rational being, he necessarily wills that all his faculties should be developed, inasmuch as they are given him and serve him for all sorts of purposes.

4. A fourth man, for whom things are going well, sees that others (whom he could help) have to struggle with great hardships, and he asks, "What concern of mine is it? Let each one be as happy as heaven wills, or as he can make himself; I will not take anything from him or even envy him; but to his welfare or to his assistance in time of need I have no desire to contribute." If such a way of thinking were a universal law of nature, certainly the human race could exist, and without doubt even better than in a state where everyone talks of sympathy and good will or even exerts himself occasionally to practice them while, on the other hand, he cheats when he can and betrays or otherwise violates the right of man. Now although it is possible that a universal law of nature according to that maxim could exist, it is nevertheless impossible to will that such a principle should hold everywhere as a law of nature. For a will which resolved this would conflict with itself, since instances can often arise in which he would need the love and sympathy of others, and in which he would have robbed himself, by such a law of nature springing from his own will, of all hope of the aid he desires.

The foregoing are a few of the many actual duties, or at least of duties we hold to be actual, whose derivation from the one stated principle is clear. We must be able to will that a 424 maxim of our action become a universal law; this is the canon of the moral estimation of our action generally. Some actions are of such a nature that their maxim cannot even be *thought* as a universal law of nature without contradiction, far from it being possible that one could will that it should be such. In others this internal impossibility is not found, though it is still impossible to *will* that that maxim should be raised to the universality of a law of nature, because such a will would contradict itself. We easily see that a maxim of the first kind conflicts with stricter or narrower (imprescriptable) duty, that of the latter with broader (meritorious) duty. Thus all duties, so far as the kind of obligation (not the object of their action) is concerned, have been completely exhibited by these examples in their dependence upon the same principle.

When we observe ourselves in any transgression of a duty, we find that we do not actually will that our maxim should become a universal law. That is impossible for us; rather, the contrary of this maxim should remain as a law generally, and we only take the liberty of making an exception to it for ourselves or for the sake of our inclination, and for this one occasion. Consequently, if we weighed everything from one and the same standpoint, namely, reason, we would come upon a contradiction in our own will, viz., that a certain principle is objectively necessary as a universal law and yet subjectively does not hold universally but rather admits exceptions. However, since we regard our action at one time from the point of view of a will wholly conformable to reason and then from that of a will affected by inclinations, there is actually no contradiction, but rather an opposition of inclination to the precept of reason (*antagonismus*). In this the universality of the principle (*universalitas*) is changed into mere generality (*generalitas*), whereby the practical principle of reason meets the maxim halfway. Although this cannot be justified in our own impartial judgment, it does show that we actually acknowledge the validity of the categorical imperative and allow ourselves (with all respect to it) only a few exceptions which seem to us to be unimportant and forced upon us.

We have thus at least established that if duty is a concept 425 which is to have significance and actual law-giving authority for our actions, it can be expressed only in categorical imperatives and not at all in hypothetical ones. For every application of it we have also clearly exhibited the content of the categorical imperative which must contain the principle of all duty (if there is such). This is itself very much. But we are not yet advanced far enough to prove a priori that that kind of imperative really exists, that there is a practical law which of itself commands absolutely and without any incentives, and that obedience to this law is duty.

With a view to attaining this, it is extremely important to remember that we must not let ourselves think that the reality of this principle can be derived from the particular constitution of human nature. For duty is practical unconditional necessity of action; it must, therefore, hold for all rational beings (to which alone an imperative can apply), and only for that reason can it be a law for all human wills. Whatever is derived from the particular natural situation of man as such, or from certain feelings and propensities, or even from a particular tendency of the human reason which might not hold necessarily for the will of every rational being (if such a tendency is possible), can give a maxim valid for us but not a law; that is, it can give a subjective principle by which we might act if only we have the propensity and inclination, but not an objective principle by which we would be directed to act even if all our propensity, inclination, and natural tendency were opposed to it. This is so far the case that the sublimity and intrinsic worth of the command is the better shown in a duty the fewer subjective causes there are for it and the more they are against it; the latter do not weaken the constraint of the law or diminish its validity.

Here we see philosophy brought to what is, in fact, a precarious position, which should be made fast even though it is supported by nothing in either heaven or earth. Here philosophy must show its purity, as the absolute sustainer of its laws, and not as the herald of laws which an implanted sense or who knows what tutelary nature whispers to it. Those may be better than nothing at all, but they can never afford fundamental principles, which reason alone dictates. These fundamental principles must originate entirely a priori and thereby obtain their commanding authority; they can expect nothing from the inclination of men but everything from the supremacy of the law and due respect for it. Otherwise they condemn man to self-contempt and inner abhorrence.

Thus everything empirical is not only wholly unworthy to be an ingredient in the principle of morality but is even highly prejudicial to the purity of moral practices themselves. For, in morals, the proper and inestimable worth of an absolutely good will consists precisely in the freedom of the principle of action from all influences from contingent grounds which only experience can furnish. We cannot too much or too often warn against the lax or even base manner of thought which seeks its principles among empirical motives and laws, for human reason in its weariness is glad to rest on this pillow. In a dream of sweet illusions (in which it embraces not Juno but a cloud), it substitutes for morality a bastard patched up from limbs of very different parentage, which looks like anything one wishes to see in it, but not like virtue to anyone who has ever beheld her in her true form.*

The question then is: Is it a necessary law for all rational beings that they should always judge their actions by such maxims as they themselves could will to serve as universal laws? If there is such a law, it must be connected wholly a priori with the concept of the will of a rational being as such. But in order to discover this connection, we must, however reluctantly, take a step into metaphysics, although in a region of it different from speculative philosophy, namely into the metaphysics of morals. In a practical philosophy it is not a   427
question of assuming grounds for what happens but of assuming laws of what ought to happen even though it may never happen (that is to say, we assume objective practical laws). Hence in practical philosophy we need not inquire into the reasons why something pleases or displeases, how the plea-

---

*To behold virtue in her proper form is nothing else than to exhibit morality stripped of all admixture of sensuous things and of every spurious adornment of reward or self-love. How much she then eclipses everything which appears charming to the senses can easily be seen by everyone with the least effort of his reason, if it be not spoiled for all abstraction.

sure of mere feeling differs from taste, and whether this is distinct from a general satisfaction of reason. Nor need we ask on what the feeling of pleasure or displeasure rests, how desires and inclinations arise, and how, finally, maxims arise from desires and inclination under the co-operation of reason. For all these matters belong to empirical psychology, which would be the second part of physics if we consider it as philosophy of nature so far as it rests on empirical laws. But here it is a question of objectively practical laws and thus of the relation of a will to itself so far as it determines itself only by reason, for everything which has a relation to the empirical automatically falls away, because if reason of itself alone determines conduct, it must necessarily do so a priori. The possibility of reason's thus determining conduct must now be investigated.

The will is thought of as a faculty of determining itself to action in accordance with the conception of certain laws. Such a faculty can be found only in rational beings. That which serves the will as the objective ground of its self-determination is a purpose, and if it is given by reason alone it must hold alike for all rational beings. On the other hand, that which contains the ground of the possibility of the action, whose result is an end, is called the means. The subjective ground of desire is the incentive (*Triebfeder*) while the objective ground of volition is the motive (*Bewegungsgrund*). Thus arises the distinction between subjective purposes, which rest on incentives, and objective purposes, which depend on motives valid for every rational being. Practical principles are formal when they disregard all subjective purposes; they are material when they have subjective purposes and thus certain incentives as their basis. The purposes that a rational being holds before himself by choice as consequences of his action are material purposes and are without exception only relative, for only their relation to a particularly constituted faculty of desire in the subject gives them their worth. And this worth cannot afford any universal principles for all rational beings or any principles valid and necessary for every volition. That is, they cannot give rise to any practical

428

laws. All these relative purposes, therefore, are grounds for hypothetical imperatives only.

But suppose that there were something the existence of which in itself had absolute worth, something which, as an end in itself, could be a ground of definite laws. In it and only in it could lie the ground of a possible categorical imperative (i.e., of a practical law).

Now, I say, man and, in general, every rational being exists as an end in himself and not merely as a means to be arbitrarily used by this or that will. In all his actions, whether they are directed toward himself or toward other rational beings, he must always be regarded at the same time as an end. All objects of inclination have only conditional worth, for if the inclinations and needs founded on them did not exist, their object would be worthless. The inclinations themselves as the sources of needs, however, are so lacking in absolute worth that the universal wish of every rational being must be indeed to free himself completely from them. Therefore, the worth of any objects to be obtained by our actions is at times conditional. Beings whose existence does not depend on our will but on nature, if they are not rational beings, have only relative worth as means, and are therefore called "things"; rational beings, on the other hand, are designated "persons" because their nature indicates that they are ends in themselves (i.e., things which may not be used merely as means). Such a being is thus an object of respect, and as such restricts all [arbitrary] choice. Such beings are not merely subjective ends whose existence as a result of our action has a worth for us, but are objective ends (i.e., beings whose existence is an end in itself). Such an end is one in the place of which no other end, to which these beings should serve merely as means, can be put. Without them, nothing of absolute worth could be found, and if all worth is conditional and thus contingent, no supreme practical principle for reason could be found anywhere.

Thus if there is to be a supreme practical principle and a categorical imperative for the human will, it must be one that forms an objective principle of the will from the conception of that which is necessarily an end for everyone because it is an end in itself. Hence this objective principle can serve as a universal law. The ground of this principle is: rational nature exists as an end in itself. Man necessarily thinks of his own existence in this way, and thus far it is a subjective principle of human actions. Also every other rational being thinks of his existence on the same rational ground which holds also for myself;* thus it is at the same time an objective principle from which, as a supreme practical ground, it must be possible to derive all laws of the will. The practical imperative, therefore, is the following: Act so that you treat humanity, whether in your own person or in that of another, always as an end and never as a means only. Let us now see whether this can be achieved. To return to our previous examples:

First, according to the concept of necessary duty to oneself, he who contemplates suicide will ask himself whether his action can be consistent with the idea of humanity as an end in itself. If in order to escape from burdensome circumstances he destroys himself, he uses a person merely as a means to maintain a tolerable condition up to the end of life. Man, however, is not a thing, and thus not something to be used merely as a means; he must always be regarded in all his actions as an end in himself. Therefore I cannot dispose of man in my own person so as to mutilate, corrupt, or kill him. (It belongs to ethics proper to define more accurately this basic principle so as to avoid all misunderstanding, e.g., as to amputating limbs in order to preserve myself, or to exposing my life to danger in order to save it; I must therefore omit them here.)

Second, as concerns necessary or obligatory duties to others, he who intends a deceitful promise to others sees immediately that he intends to use another man merely as a means, without the latter at the same time containing the end in himself. For he whom I want to use for my own purposes by means of such a promise cannot possibly assent to my

* Here I present this proposition as a postulate, but in the last Section grounds for it will be found.

mode of acting against him and thus share in the purpose of this action. This conflict with the principle of other men is even clearer if we cite examples of attacks on their freedom and property, for then it is clear that he who violates the rights of men intends to make use of the person of others merely as means, without considering that, as rational beings, they must always be esteemed at the same time as ends (i.e., only as beings who must be able to embody in themselves the purpose of the very same action).*

Thirdly, with regard to contingent (meritorious) duty to oneself, it is not sufficient that the action not conflict with humanity in our person as an end in itself; it must also harmonize with it. In humanity there are capacities for greater perfection which belong to the purpose of nature with respect to humanity in our own person, and to neglect these might perhaps be consistent with the preservation of humanity as an end in itself, but not with the furtherance of that end.

Fourthly, with regard to meritorious duty to others, the natural purpose that all men have is their own happiness. Humanity might indeed exist if no one contributed to the happiness of others, provided he did not intentionally detract from it, but this harmony with humanity as an end in itself is only negative, not positive, if everyone does not also endeavor, as far as he can, to further the purposes of others. For the ends of any person, who is an end in himself, must as far as possible be also my ends, if that conception of an end in itself is to have its full effect on me.

This principle of humanity, and in general of every rational   431
creature an end in itself, is the supreme limiting condition on

*Let it not be thought that the banal "what you do not wish to be done to you . . ." could here serve as guide or principle, for it is only derived from the principle and is restricted by various limitations. It cannot be a universal law, because it contains the ground neither of duties to one's self nor of the benevolent duties to others (for many a man would gladly consent that others should not benefit him, provided only that he might be excused from showing benevolence to them). Nor does it contain the ground of obligatory duties to another, for the criminal would argue on this ground against the judge who sentences him. And so on.

the freedom of action of each man. It is not borrowed from experience, first, because of its universality, since it applies to all rational beings generally, and experience does not suffice to determine anything about them; and secondly, because in experience humanity is not thought of (subjectively) as the purpose of men (i.e., as an object which we of ourselves really make our purpose). Rather it is thought of as the objective end which ought to constitute the supreme limiting condition of all subjective ends whatever they may be. Thus this principle must arise from pure reason. Objectively the ground of all practical legislation lies (according to the first principle) in the rule and form of universality, which makes it capable of being a law (at least a natural law); subjectively it lies in the end. But the subject of all ends is every rational being as an end in itself (by the second principle); from this there follows the third practical principle of the will as the supreme condition of its harmony with universal practical reason, viz, the Idea of the will of every rational being as making universal law.

By this principle all maxims are rejected which are not consistent with the will's giving universal law. The will is not only subject to the law, but subject in such a way that it must be conceived also as itself prescribing the law, of which reason can hold itself to be the author; it is on this ground alone that the will is regarded as subject to the law.

By the very fact that the imperatives are thought of as categorical, either way of conceiving them—as imperatives demanding the lawfulness of actions, resembling the lawfulness of the natural order; or as imperatives of the universal prerogative of the purposes of rational beings as such— excludes from their sovereign authority all admixture of any interest as an incentive to obedience. But we have been *assuming* the imperatives to be categorical, for that was necessary if we wished to explain the concept of duty; that there are practical propositions which command categorically could not of itself be proved independently, just as little as it can be proved anywhere in this section. One thing, however could have been done: to indicate in the imperative itself, by some

determination inherent in it, that i[n]
renunciation of all interest is the specific
cal imperative, distinguishing it from the h[y]
this is now done in the third formulation of the p
in the Idea of the will of every rational being as a
universal law. A will which is subject to laws can be b[ound]
them by an interest, but a will giving the supreme law ca[n]
possibly depend upon any interest, for such a dependent wil[l]
would itself need still another law which would restrict the
interest of its self-love to the condition that its [maxim] should
be valid as a universal law.

Thus the principle of every human will as a will giving
universal law in all its maxims* is very well adapted to being a
categorical imperative, provided it is otherwise correct. Because of the Idea of giving universal law, it is based on no
interest; and thus of all possible imperatives, it alone can be
unconditional. Or, better, converting the proposition: if there
is a categorical imperative (a law for the will of every rational
being), it can command only that everything be done from
the maxim of its will as one which could have as its object
only itself considered as giving universal law. For only in this
case are the practical principle and the imperative which the
will obeys unconditional, because the will can have no interest as its foundation.

If now we look back upon all previous attempts which have
ever been undertaken to discover the principle of morality, it
is not to be wondered at that they all had to fail. Man was seen
to be bound to laws by his duty, but it was not seen that he is
subject to his own, but still universal, legislation, and that he
is bound to act only in accordance with his own will, which is,
however, designed by nature to be a will giving universal law.
For if one thought of him as only subject to a law (whatever it
may be), this necessarily implied some interest as a stimulus
or compulsion to obedience because the law did not arise   433
from his will. Rather, his will had to be constrained by some-

---

* I may be excused from citing examples to elucidate this principle,
for those that have already illustrated the categorical imperative and its
formula can here serve the same purpose.

this strictly necessary
of finding a supreme
nd one never arrived at
from a certain interest.
of another, but in either
e conditional, and could
id. The moral principle I
y of the will in contrast to
accordingly count under

being as a being that must
aw through all the maxims of
self and its actions from this
tful concept, namely that of a

it□
standpoint, ... *realm of ends*.

By *realm* I understand the systematic union of different rational beings through common laws. Because laws determine which ends have universal validity, if we abstract from personal differences of rational beings, and thus from all content of their private purposes, we can think of a whole of all ends in systematic connection, a whole of rational beings as ends in themselves as well as a whole of particular purposes which each may set for himself. This is a realm of ends, which is possible on the principles stated above. For all rational beings stand under the law that each of them should treat himself and all others never merely as means, but in every case at the same time as an end in himself. Thus there arises a systematic union of rational beings through common objective laws. This is a realm which may be called a realm of ends (certainly only an ideal) because what these laws have in view is just the relation of these beings to each other as ends and means.

434 A rational being belongs to the realm of ends as a member when he gives universal laws in it while also himself subject to these laws. He belongs to it as sovereign when, as legislating, he is subject to the will of no other. The rational being must regard himself always as legislative in a realm of ends possible through the freedom of the will whether he belongs

to it as member or as sovereign. He cannot maintain his position as sovereign merely through the maxims of his will, but only when he is a completely independent being without need and with unlimited power adequate to his will.

Morality, therefore, consists in the relation of every action to the legislation through which alone a realm of ends is possible. This legislation must be found in every rational being. It must be able to arise from his will, whose principle then is to do no action according to any maxim which would be inconsistent with its being a universal law, and thus to act only so that the will through its maxims could regard itself at the same time as giving universal law. If the maxims do not by their nature already necessarily conform to this objective principle of rational beings as giving universal law, the necessity of acting according to that principle is called practical constraint, which is to say: duty. Duty pertains not to the sovereign of the realm of ends, but rather to each member and to each in the same degree.

The practical necessity of acting according to this principle (duty) does not rest at all on feelings, impulses, and inclinations; it rests solely on the relation of rational beings to one another, in which the will of a rational being must always be regarded as legislative, for otherwise it could not be thought of as an end in itself. Reason, therefore, relates every maxim of the will as giving universal laws to every other will and also to every action towards itself; it does not do so for the sake of any other practical motive or future advantage but rather from the Idea of the dignity of a rational being who obeys no law except one which he himself also gives.

In the realm of ends everything has either a *price* or a *dignity*. Whatever has a price can be replaced by something else as its equivalent; on the other hand, whatever is above all price and therefore admits of no equivalent, has dignity.

That which is related to general human inclinations and needs has a *market price*. That which, without presupposing any need, accords with a certain taste (i.e., with pleasure in the purposeless play of our faculties) has a *fancy price*. But that which constitutes the condition under which alone some-

435

thing can be an end in itself does not have mere relative worth (price) but an intrinsic worth (*dignity*).

Morality is the condition under which alone a rational being can be an end in himself, because only through it is it possible to be a lawgiving member in the realm of ends. Thus morality, and humanity so far as it is capable of morality, alone have dignity. Skill and diligence in work have a market value; wit, lively imagination, and humor have a fancy price; but fidelity in promises and benevolence on principle (not benevolence from instinct) have intrinsic worth. Nature and likewise art contain nothing which could make up for their lack, for their worth consists not in the effects which flow from them nor in any advantage and utility which they procure; it consists only in mental dispositions, maxims of the will, which are ready to reveal themselves in this manner through actions even though success does not favor them. These actions need no recommendation from my subjective disposition or taste in order that they may be looked upon with immediate favor and satisfaction, nor do they have need of any direct propensity or feeling directed to them. They exhibit the will which performs them as the object of an immediate respect, since nothing but reason is required in order to impose them upon the will. The will is not to be cajoled into them, for this, in the case of duties, would be a contradiction. This esteem lets the worth of such a turn of mind be recognized as dignity and puts it infinitely beyond any price; with things of price it cannot in the least be brought into any competition or comparison without, as it were, violating its holiness.

And what is it that justifies the morally good disposition or virtue in making such lofty claims? It is nothing less that the participation it affords the rational being in giving universal laws. He is thus fitted to be a member in a possible realm of ends, to which his own nature already destined him. For, as an end in himself, he is destined to be a lawgiver in the realm of ends, free from all laws of nature and obedient only to those laws which he himself gives. Accordingly, his maxims can belong to a universal legislation to which he is at the same time subject. A thing has no worth other than that determined for it by the law. The lawgiving which determines all worth must therefore have a dignity (i.e., an unconditional and incomparable worth). For the esteem which a rational being must have for it, only the word "respect"* is suitable. Autonomy is thus the basis of the dignity of both human nature and every rational nature.

The three aforementioned ways of presenting the principle of morality are fundamentally only so many formulas of the very same law, and each of them unites the others in itself. There is, nevertheless, a difference between them, but the difference is more subjectively than objectively practical, for the difference is intended to bring an Idea of reason closer to intuition (by means of a certain analogy) and thus nearer to feeling. All maxims have:

1. A form, which consists in universality, and in this respect the formula of the moral imperative requires that maxims be chosen as though they should hold as universal laws of nature.
2. A material (i.e., an end), and in this respect the formula says that the rational being, as by its nature an end and thus as an end in itself, must serve in every maxim as the condition restricting all merely relative and arbitrary ends.
3. A complete determination of all maxims by the formula that all maxims which stem from autonomous legislation ought to harmonize with a possible realm of ends as with a realm of nature.†

---

*H.J. Paton, in his translation of this text, prefers to translate the German word *Achtung* as *reverence*. There are religious overtones of awe before the sublimity of the moral law which speak in favor of Paton's choice.

†Teleology considers nature as a realm of ends; morals regards a possible realm of ends as a realm of nature. In the former the realm of ends is a theoretical Idea for the explanation of what actually is. In the latter it is a practical Idea for bringing about that which does not exist but which can become actual through our conduct and for making it conform with this Idea.

There is a progression here like that through the categories of the unity of the form of the will (its universality), the plurality of material (the objects, ends), to the all-comprehensiveness or totality of the system of ends. But it is better in moral valuation to follow the rigorous method and to make 437 the universal formula of the categorical imperative the basis: Act according to the maxim which can at the same time make itself a universal law. But if one wishes to gain a hearing for the moral law, it is very useful to bring one and the same action under the three stated principles and thus, so far as possible, bring it nearer to intuition.

We can now end where we started, with the concept of an unconditionally good will. That will is absolutely good which cannot be bad, and thus it is a will whose maxim, when made universal law, can never conflict with itself. Thus this principle is also its supreme law: Always act according to that maxim whose universality as law you can at the same time will. This is the only condition under which a will can never come into conflict with itself, and such an imperative is categorical. Because the validity of the will as a universal law for possible actions has an analogy with the universal connection of the existence of things under universal laws, which is the formal element of nature in general, the categorical imperative can be expressed also as follows: Act on those maxims which can at the same time have themselves as universal laws of nature as their object. Such, then, is the formula of an absolutely good will.

Rational nature is distinguished from others in that it proposes an end to itself. This end would be the material of every good will. Since, however, in the Idea of an absolutely good will without the limiting condition that this or that end be achieved, we must abstract from every end to be actually effected (as any particular end would make each will only relatively good), we must conceive the end here not as one to be brought about, but as a self-existent end, and thus merely negatively, as that which must never be acted against and which consequently must never be valued merely as a means but in every volition also as an end. Now this end can never be other than the subject of all possible ends themselves, because this is at the same time the subject of a possible will which is absolutely good, for the latter cannot without contradiction be made secondary to any other object. The principle: Act with reference to every rational being (whether yourself or another) so that in your maxim it is an end in itself, is thus basically identical with the principle: Act by a maxim which involves its own universal validity for every rational being.

That in the use of means to any end I should restrict my maxim to the condition of its universal validity as a law for every subject is tantamount to saying that the subject of ends (i.e., the rational being itself) must be made the basis of all 438 maxims of actions and thus be treated never as a mere means but as the supreme limiting condition in the use of all means (i.e., as at the same time an end).

It follows incontestably that every rational being must be able to regard himself as an end in himself with reference to all laws to which he may be subject whatever they may be, and thus see himself as giving universal laws. For it is just the fitness of his maxims to universal legislation that indicates that he is an end in himself. It also follows that his dignity (his prerogative) over all merely natural beings entails that he must take his maxims from the point of view that regards himself, and hence also every other rational being, as legislative. Rational beings are, on this account, called persons. In this way, a world of rational beings (*mundus intelligibilis*) is possible as a realm of ends, because of the legislation belonging to all persons as members. Consequently every rational being must act as if by his maxims he were at all times a legislative member of the universal realm of ends. The formal principle of these maxims is: So act as if your maxims should serve at the same time as universal law (for all rational beings).

A realm of ends is thus possible only by analogy with a realm of nature. The former is possible only by maxims (i.e., self-imposed rules), while the latter is possible by laws of efficient causes of things externally necessitated. Regardless of this difference, by analogy we call the natural whole a realm of nature so far as it is related to rational beings as its end; we do so even though the natural whole is looked upon as a machine. Such a realm of ends would actually be realized through maxims whose rule is prescribed to all rational beings by the categorical imperative, if they were universally obeyed. But a rational being, though he scrupulously follow this maxim, cannot for that reason expect every other rational being to be true to it, nor can he expect the realm of nature and its orderly design to harmonize with him as a fitting member of a realm of ends which is possible through himself. That is, he cannot count on its favoring his expectation of happiness. Still the law: Act according to the maxim of a member of a merely potential realm of ends who gives universal law, remains in full force because it commands categorically. And just in this lies the paradox that simply the dignity of humanity as rational nature without any end or advantage to be gained by it, and thus respect for a mere Idea, should serve as the inflexible precept of the will. [There is the further paradox that] the sublimity of the maxims and the worthiness of every rational subject to be a law-giving member in the realm of ends consist precisely in the independence of his maxims from all such incentives. Otherwise he would have to be viewed as subject to only the natural law of his needs. Although the realm of nature as well as that of ends would be thought of as united under a sovereign, so that the latter would no longer remain a mere Idea but would receive true reality, the realm of ends would undoubtedly gain a strong urge in its favor though its intrinsic worth would not be augmented. Regardless of this, even the one and only absolute legislator would still have to be conceived as judging the worth of rational beings only by the disinterested conduct which they prescribe to themselves merely from the Idea. The essence of things is not changed by their external relations, and without reference to these relations a man must be judged only by what constitutes his absolute worth, and this is true whoever his judge may be, even if it be the Supreme Being. Morality is thus the relation of actions to the autonomy of the will (i.e., to the possible giving of universal law by the maxims of the will). The action which can be compatible with the autonomy of the will is permitted; that which does not agree with it is prohibited. The will whose maxims are necessarily in harmony with the laws of autonomy is a holy will or an absolutely good will. The dependence of a will not absolutely good on the principle of autonomy (moral constraint) is *obligation*. Hence obligation cannot be predicated of a holy will. The objective necessity of an action from obligation is called *duty*.

From what has just been said, it can easily be explained how it happens that, although in the concept of duty we think of subjection to law, we do nevertheless at the same time ascribe a certain sublimity and dignity to the person who $\qquad$ 440 fulfills all his duties. For though there is no sublimity in him in so far as he is subject to the moral law, yet he is sublime in so far as he is the giver of the law and subject to it for this reason only. We have also shown above how neither fear of nor inclination to the law is the incentive which can give moral worth to action; only respect for it can do so. Our own will, so far as it would act only under the condition of a universal legislation rendered possible by its maxims — this will ideally possible for us — is the proper object of respect, and the dignity of humanity consists just in its capacity to give universal laws under the condition that it is itself subject to this same legislation.

The Autonomy of the Will as the Supreme Principle of Morality

Autonomy of the will is that property of it by which it is a law to itself independent of any property of the objects of its volition. Hence the principle of autonomy is: Never choose except in such a way that the maxims of the choice are comprehended as universal law in the same volition. That this practical rule is an imperative, that is, that the will of every rational being is necessarily bound to it as a condition, cannot be proved by a mere analysis of the concepts occurring in it, because it is a synthetical proposition. To prove it, we would have to go beyond the knowledge of objects to a critical examination of the subject (i.e., to a critique of pure practical reason), for this synthetical proposition which commands apodictically must be susceptible of being known a priori. This matter, however, does not belong in the present section. But that the principle of autonomy, which is now in question, is the sole principle of morals can be readily shown by mere analysis of the concepts of morality; for by this analysis we find that its principle must be a categorical imperative and that the imperative commands neither more nor less than this very autonomy.

441 **The Heteronomy of the Will as the Source of All Spurious Principles of Morality**

If the will seeks the law which is to determine it elsewhere than in the fitness of its maxims to be given as universal law, and if thus it goes outside and seeks the law in the property of any of its objects, heteronomy always results. For then the will does not give itself the law, but the object through its relation to the will gives the law to it. This relation, whether it rests on inclination or on conceptions of reason, admits of only hypothetical imperatives: I should do something for the reason that I will something else. The moral (categorical) imperative, on the other hand, says that I should act in this or that way even though I have not willed anything else. For example, the former says that I should not lie if I wish to keep my good name. The latter says that I should not lie even though it would not cause me the least injury. The latter, therefore, must disregard every object to such an extent that it has absolutely no influence on the will; it must so disregard it that practical reason (will) may not just minister to any interest not its own but rather show its commanding authority as the supreme legislation. Thus, for instance, I should seek to further the happiness of others, not as though its realization were of consequence to me (because of a direct inclination or some satisfaction related to it indirectly through reason); I should do so solely because the maxim which excludes it from my duty cannot be comprehended as a universal law in one and the same volition.

Classification of All Possible Principles of Morality Following from the Assumed Principle of Heteronomy

Here as everywhere in the pure use of reason so long as a critical examination of it is lacking, human reason tries all possible wrong ways before it succeeds in finding the one true way.

All principles which can be taken from this point of view   442
are either empirical or rational. The former, drawn from the principles of happiness, are based on physical or moral feeling; the latter, drawn from the principle of perfection, are based either on the rational concept of perfection as a possible result or on the concept of an independent perfection (the will of God) as the determining ground of the will.

Empirical principles are not at all suited to serve as the basis of moral laws. For if the basis of the universality by which they should be valid for all rational beings without distinction (the unconditional practical necessity which is thereby imposed upon them) is derived from a particular tendency of human nature or the accidental circumstance in which it is found, that universality is lost. But the principle of one's own happiness is the most objectionable of the empirical principles. This is not merely because it is false and because experience contradicts the supposition that well-being is always proportional to good conduct, nor yet because this principle contributes nothing to the establishment of morality inasmuch as it is a very different thing to make a man happy from making him good, and to make him prudent and far-sighted for his own advantage is far from making him virtuous. Rather, it is because this principle supports morality with incentives which undermine it and destroy all its sublimity, for it puts the motives to virtue and those to vice in the same class, teaching us only to make a better calculation while obliterating the specific difference between them. On the other hand, there is the alleged special sense,* the moral feeling. The appeal to it is superficial, since those who cannot think expect help from feeling, even with respect to that which concerns universal laws; they do so even though feelings naturally differ so infinitely in degree that they are incapable of furnishing a uniform standard of the good and bad, and also in spite of the fact that one cannot validly judge for others by means of one's own feeling. Nevertheless, the moral feeling is nearer to morality and its dignity, inasmuch as it pays virtue the honor of ascribing the satisfaction and esteem for her directly to morality, and does not, as it were, say to her face that it is not her beauty but only our advantage which attaches us to her.

443 Among the rational principles of morality, there is the ontological concept of perfection. It is empty, indefinite, and consequently useless for finding in the immeasurable field of possible reality the greatest possible sum which is suitable to us; and, in specifically distinguishing the reality which is here in question from all other reality, it inevitably tends to move in a circle and cannot avoid tacitly presupposing the morality which it ought to explain. Nevertheless, it is better than the theological concept, which derives morality from a most perfect divine will. It is better not merely because we cannot intuit the perfection of the divine will, having rather to derive it only from our own concepts of which morality itself is foremost, but also because if we do not so derive it (and to do so would involve a most flagrant circle in explanation), the only remaining concept of the divine will is made up of the attributes of desire for glory and dominion combined with the

---

*I count the principle of moral feeling under that of happiness, because every empirical interest promises to contribute to our well-being by the agreeableness that a thing affords, either directly and without a view to future advantage or with a view to it. We must likewise, with Hutcheson, count the principle of sympathy with the happiness of others under the moral sense which he assumed.

awful conceptions of might and vengeance, and any system of ethics based on them would be directly opposed to morality.

But if I had to choose between the concept of the moral sense and that of perfection in general (neither of which at any rate weakens morality, though neither is capable of serving as its foundation), I would decide for the latter, because it preserves the indefinite Idea of a will good in itself free from corruption until it can be more narrowly defined. It at least withdraws the decision on the question from the realm of sensibility and brings it to the court of pure reason, although it does not even there decide the question.

For the rest, I think I may be excused from a lengthy refutation of all these doctrines. It is so easy, and presumably so well understood even by those whose office requires them to decide for one of these theories (since their students would not tolerate suspension of judgment), that such a refutation would be superfluous. What interests us more, however, is to know that all these principles set up nothing other than heteronomy of the will as the first ground of morality, and thus they necessarily miss their goal.

In every case in which the object of the will must be 444 assumed as prescribing the rule which is to determine the will, the rule is nothing else than heteronomy. The imperative in this case is conditional, stating that if or because one wills such and such an object, one ought to act thus or so. Therefore the imperative can never command morally, that is, categorically. The object may determine the will by means of inclination, as in the principle of one's own happiness, or by means of reason directed to objects of our possible volition in general, as in the principle of perfection; but the will in these cases never determines itself directly by the conception of the action itself but only by the incentive which the foreseen result of the action incites in the will—that is: I ought to do something because I will something else. And here still another law must be assumed in me as the basis for this imperative; it would be a law by which I would necessarily will that other thing; but this law would in its turn require an imperative to restrict this maxim. Since the conception of a result to be obtained by one's own powers incites in the will an impulse which depends upon the natural characteristic of the subject, either of his sensibility (inclination and taste) or understanding and reason; and since these faculties according to the particular constitution of their nature find satisfaction in exercising themselves on the result of the voluntary action, it follows that it would really be nature which would give the law [to the action]. This law, as a law of nature, would have to be known and proved by experience, and as in itself contingent it would be unfit to be an apodictical practical rule such as the moral rule must be. Such a law always represents heteronomy of the will: the will does not give itself the law, but an external impulse gives the law to the will according to nature of the subject which is susceptible to receive it.

The absolutely good will, the principle of which must be a categorical imperative, is thus undetermined with reference to any object. It contains only the form of volition in general, and this form is autonomy. That is, the capability of the maxims of every good will to make themselves universal laws is itself the sole law which the will of every rational being imposes on himself, and it does not need to support this by any incentive or interest.

How such a synthetical practical a priori proposition is possible and why it is necessary is a problem whose solution does not lie within the boundaries of the metaphysics of morals. Moreover, we have not here affirmed its truth, and even less professed to command a proof of it. We showed only through the development of the generally received concept of morals that autonomy of the will is unavoidably connected with it, or rather that it is its foundation. Whoever, therefore, holds morality to be something real and not a chimerical idea without truth must also concede its principle which has been derived here. Consequently, this section, like the first, was merely analytical. To prove that morality is not a mere phantom of the mind—and if the categorical imperative, and with it the autonomy of the will, is true and absolutely necessary as an a priori proposition, it follows that it is no phantom—requires that a synthetical use of pure practical reason be possible. But we must not venture on this use without first making a critical examination of this faculty of reason. In the last section we shall give the principal features of such an examination that will be sufficient for our purpose.

Third Section
Transition from the Metaphysics of Morals to the Critical Examination of Pure Practical Reason[4]

The Concept of Freedom Is the Key to the Explanation of the Autonomy of the Will

As will is a kind of causality of living beings so far as they are rational, freedom would be that property of this causality by which it can be effective independent of foreign causes determining it, just as natural necessity is the property of the causality of all irrational beings by which they are determined to activity by the influence of foreign causes. 446

The preceding definition of freedom is negative and therefore affords no insight into its essence. But a positive concept of freedom flows from it which is so much the richer and more fruitful. Since the concept of a causality entails that of laws according to which something (i.e., the effect) must be established through something else which we call cause, it follows that freedom is by no means lawless even though it is not a property of the will according to laws of nature. Rather, it must be a causality of a peculiar kind according to immutable laws. Otherwise a free will would be an absurdity. Natural necessity is, as we have seen, a heteronomy of efficient

---

[4]*Kritik der reinen praktischen Vernunft.* These words do not refer to the book, *Critique of Practical Reason.* At the time Kant wrote the *Foundations of the Metaphysics of Morals* he did not anticipate writing a second *Critique* but planned to go directly to the composition of the *Metaphysics of Morals* (first published in 1797).

causes, for every effect is possible only according to the law that something else determines the efficient cause to its causality. What else, then, can the freedom of the will be but autonomy (i.e., the property of the will to be law to itself)? The proposition that the will is a law to itself in all its actions, however, only expresses the principle that we should act according to no other maxim than that which can also have itself as a universal law for its object. And this is just the formula of the categorical imperative and the principle of morality. Therefore a free will and a will under moral laws are identical.

Thus if freedom of the will is presupposed, morality together with its principle follows from it by the mere analysis of its concepts. But the principle: An absolutely good will is one whose maxim can always include itself as a universal law, is nevertheless a synthetical proposition. It is synthetical because by analysis of the concept of an absolutely good will that property of the maxim cannot be found in it. Such synthetical propositions, however, are made possible only by the fact that the two cognitions are connected with each other through their union with a third in which both are to be found. The positive concept of freedom furnishes this third cognition, which cannot be, as in the case of physical causes, the sensible world of nature, in the concept of which we find conjoined the concepts of something as cause in relation to something else as effect. We cannot yet show directly what this third cognition is to which freedom directs us and of which we have an a priori Idea, nor can we yet explain the deduction of the concept of freedom from pure practical reason, and therewith the possibility of a categorical imperative. For this, some further preparation is needed.

Freedom Must be Presupposed as the Property of the Will of All Rational Beings

It is not enough to ascribe freedom to our will, on whatever grounds, if we do not also have sufficient grounds for attributing it to all rational beings. For since morality serves as a law for us only as rational beings, it must hold for all rational beings, and since it must be derived exclusively from the property of freedom, freedom as a property of the will of all rational beings must be demonstrated. And it does not suffice 448 to prove it from certain alleged experiences of human nature (which is indeed impossible, as it can be proved only a priori), but we must prove it as belonging universally to the activity of rational beings endowed with a will. Now I say that every being which cannot act otherwise than under the Idea of freedom is thereby really free in a practical respect. That is to say, all laws which are inseparably bound with freedom hold for it just as if its wills were proved free in itself by theoretical philosophy.* Now I affirm that we must necessarily grant that every rational being who has a will also has the Idea of freedom and that it acts only under this Idea. For in such a being we think of a reason which is practical (i.e., a reason which has causality with respect to its object). Now we cannot conceive of a reason which, in making its judgments, consciously responds to a bidding from the outside, for then the subject would attribute the determination of its power of judgment not to reason but to an impulse. Reason must regard itself as the author of its principles, independently of alien influences; consequently as practical reason or as the will of a rational being it must regard itself as free. That is to say, the will of a rational being can be a will of its own only under the Idea of freedom, and therefore from a practical point of view such a will must be ascribed to all rational beings.

---

*I propose this argument as sufficient to our purpose: Freedom as an Idea is posited by all rational beings as the basis for their actions. I do so in order to avoid having to prove freedom also in its theoretical aspect. For even if the latter is left unproved, the laws which would obligate a being who was really free would hold for a being who cannot act except under the Idea of his own freedom. Thus we escape the onus which has been pressed on theory.

Of the Interest Attaching to the Ideas
of Morality

We have finally reduced the definite concept of morality to the Idea of freedom, but we could not prove freedom to be actual in ourselves and in human nature. We saw only that we
449 must presuppose it if we would think of a being as rational and conscious of its causality with respect to actions, that is, as endowed with a will; and so we find that on the very same grounds we must ascribe to each being endowed with reason and will the property of determining itself to action under the Idea of its freedom.

From presupposing this Idea [of freedom] there followed also the consciousness of a law of action: that the subjective principles of actions (i.e., maxims) must in every instance be so chosen that they can hold also as objective (i.e., universal) principles, and can thus serve as principles for our giving universal laws. But why should I, as a rational being, and why should all other beings endowed with reason, subject ourselves to this law? I will admit that no interest impels me to do so, for that would then give no categorical imperative. But I must nevertheless take an interest in it and see how it comes about, for this *ought* is properly a *would* that is valid for every rational being provided reason were practical for it without hindrance [i.e., exclusively determined its action]. For beings who, like ourselves, are affected by the senses as incentives different from reason, and who do not always do that which reason by itself alone would have done, that necessity of action is expressed as only an *ought*. The subjective necessity is thus distinguished from the objective.

It therefore seems that we have only presupposed the moral law, the principle of the autonomy of the will in the Idea of freedom, as if we could not prove its reality and objective necessity by itself. Even if that were so, we would still have gained something because we would at least have defined the genuine principle more accurately than had been done before; but with regard to its validity and the practical necessity of subjection to it, we would not have advanced a single step, for we could give no satisfactory answer to any-one who asked us why the universal validity of our maxim as a law had to be the restricting condition of our action. We could not tell on what is based the worth which we ascribe to actions of this kind—a worth so great that there can be no higher interest—nor could we tell how it happens that man believes that it is only through this that he feels his own personal worth, in contrast to which the worth of a pleasant or unpleasant state is to be regarded as nothing.

We do find sometimes that we can take an interest in a personal quality which involves no [personal] interest in any [external] condition, provided only that the [possession of] this quality makes us fit to participate in the [desired] condition in case reason were to effect the allotment of this condition. That is, being worthy of happiness, even without the motive of partaking in happiness, can interest of itself. But this judgment is in fact only the effect of the importance already ascribed to moral laws (if by the Idea of freedom we detach ourselves from every empirical interest). But that we ought so to detach ourselves from every empirical interest, to regard ourselves as free in acting and yet as subject to certain laws, in order to find a worth wholly in our person which would compensate for the loss of everything which could make our situation desirable—how this is possible and hence on what grounds the moral law obligates us still cannot be seen in this way.

We must openly confess that there is a kind of circle here from which it seems that there is no escape. We assume that we are free in the order of efficient causes so that we can conceive of ourselves as subject to moral laws in the order of ends. And then we think of ourselves subject to these laws because we have ascribed freedom of the will to ourselves. This is circular because freedom and self-legislation of the will are both autonomy and thus are reciprocal concepts, and for that reason one of them cannot be used to explain the other and to furnish a ground for it. At most they can be used for the logical purpose of bringing apparently different conceptions of the same object under a single concept (as we reduce different fractions of the same value to the lowest common terms).

One recourse, however, remains open to us, namely, to inquire whether we do not assume a different standpoint when we think of ourselves as causes a priori efficient through freedom from that which we occupy when we conceive of ourselves in the light of our actions as effects which we see before our eyes.

The following remark requires no subtle reflection, and we may suppose that even the commonest understanding can make it, though it does so, after its fashion, by an obscure discernment of judgment which it calls feeling: all conceptions, like those of the senses, which come to us without our choice enable us to know objects only as they affect us, while what they are in themselves remains unknown to us; therefore, as regards this kind of conception, even with the closest attention and clearness which understanding may ever bring to them we can attain only a knowledge of appearances and never a knowledge of things as they are in themselves. When this distinction is once made (perhaps merely because of a difference noticed between conceptions which are given to us from somewhere else and to which we are passive, and those which we produce from ourselves only and in which we show our own activity), it follows of itself that we must admit and assume behind the appearances something else which is not appearance, i.e., things as they are in themselves, although we must admit that we cannot approach them more closely and can never know what they are in themselves, since they can never be known by us except as they affect us. This must furnish a distinction, though a crude one, between a world of sense and a world of understanding. The former, by differences in our sensible faculties, can be very different to various observers, while the latter, which is its foundation, remains always the same. A man may not presume to know even himself as he really is by knowing himself through inner sensation. For since he does not, as it were, produce himself or derive his concept of himself a priori but only empirically, it is natural that he obtain his knowledge of himself through inner sense and consequently only through the appearance of his nature and the way in which his consciousness is affected. But beyond the characteristic of his own subject which is compounded of these mere appearances, he necessarily assumes something else as its basis, namely, his ego as it is in itself. Thus in respect to mere perception and receptivity to sensations he must count himself as belonging to the world of sense; but in respect to that which may be pure activity in himself (i.e., in respect to that which reaches consciousness directly and not by affecting the senses) he must reckon himself as belonging to the intellectual world. But he has no further knowledge of that world.

To such a conclusion the thinking man must come with respect to all things which may present themselves to him. Presumably it is to be met with in the commonest understanding which, as is well known, is very much inclined to expect behind the objects of the senses something else invisible and acting of itself. But common understanding soon spoils it by trying to make the invisible again sensible (i.e., to make it an object of intuition). Thus the common understanding becomes not in the least wiser.

Now man really finds in himself a faculty by which he distinguishes himself from all other things, even from himself so far as he is affected by objects. This faculty is reason. As a pure, spontaneous activity it is elevated even above understanding. For though the latter is also a spontaneous activity and does not, like sense, which is passive, merely contain representations which arise only when one is affected by things, it cannot produce by its activity any other concepts than those which serve to bring the sensible representations under rules and thereby to unite them in one consciousness. Without this use of sensibility it would think nothing at all; on the other hand, reason shows such a pure spontaneity in the case of Ideas that it[5] far transcends anything that sensibility can give to consciousness, and shows its chief occupation in

[5]Reading *sie . . . ihm* (in Cassirer ed.) instead of *sie . . . ihr* (Akademie ed.)

distinguishing the world of sense from the world of understanding, thereby prescribing limits to the understanding
itself.

For this reason a rational being must regard itself *qua*
intelligence (and not from the side of his lower faculties) as
belonging to the world of understanding and not to that of the
senses. Thus it has two standpoints from which it can consider itself and recognize the laws [governing] the employment of its powers and all its actions: first, as belonging to the
world of sense, under the laws of nature (heteronomy), and,
second, as belonging to the intelligible world under laws
which, independent of nature, are not empirical but founded
on reason alone.

As a rational being and thus as belonging to the intelligible
world, man cannot think of the causality of his own will
except under the Idea of freedom, for independence from the
determining causes of the world of sense (an independence
which reason must always ascribe to itself) is freedom. The
453 concept of autonomy is inseparably connected with the Idea
of freedom, and with the former there is inseparably bound
the universal principle of morality, which is the ground in
Idea of all actions of rational beings, just as natural law is the
ground of all appearances.

We have now removed the suspicion which we raised that
there might be a hidden circle in our reasoning from freedom
to autonomy and from the latter to the moral law. This suspicion was that we laid down the Idea of freedom for the sake of
the moral law in order later to derive the law from freedom,
and that we were thus unable to give any basis for the law,
presenting it only as a *petitio principii* which well-disposed
minds might gladly allow us, but which we could never advance as a demonstrable proposition. But we now see that, if
we think of ourselves as free, we transport ourselves into the
intelligible world as members of it and know the autonomy of
the will together with its consequence, morality; whereas if
we think of ourselves as obligated, we consider ourselves as
belonging both to the world of sense and at the same time to
the intelligible world.

How Is a Categorical Imperative Possible?

The rational being counts himself, *qua* intelligence, as belonging to the intelligible world, and only as an efficient cause belonging to it does he call his causality will. On the other side, however, he is conscious of himself as a part of the world of sense in which his actions are found as mere appearances of that causality. But we do not discern how they are possible on the basis of that causality which we do not know; rather, those actions must be regarded as determined by other appearances, namely, desires and inclinations belonging to the world of sense. As a member of the intelligible world only, all my actions would completely accord with the principle of the autonomy of the pure will, and as a part only of the world of sense would they have to be assumed to conform wholly to the natural law of desires and inclinations and thus to the heteronomy of nature. (The former actions would rest on the supreme principle of morality, and the latter on that of happiness.) But since the intelligible world contains the ground of the world of sense and hence of its laws, the intelligible world is (and must be conceived as) directly legislative for my will, which belongs wholly to the intelligible world. Therefore I recognize myself *qua* intelligence as subject to the law of the world of understanding and to the autonomy of the will. That is, I recognize myself as subject to the law of reason which contains in the Idea of freedom the law of the intelligible world, while at the same time I must acknowledge that I am a being which belongs to the world of sense. Therefore I must regard the laws of the intelligible world as imperatives for me, and actions in accord with this principle as duties.

Thus categorical imperatives are possible because the Idea of freedom makes me a member of an intelligible world. Consequently, if I were a member of that world only, all my actions *would* always be in accordance with the autonomy of the will. But since I intuit myself at the same time as a member of the world of sense, my actions *ought* to conform

454

to it, and this categorical "ought" presents a synthetic a priori proposition, since besides my will affected by my sensuous desires there is added the Idea of exactly the same will as pure, practical of itself, and belonging to the intelligible world, which according to reason contains the supreme condition of the sensuously affected will. It is similar to the manner in which concepts of the understanding, which of themselves mean nothing but lawful form in general, are added to the intuitions of the sensible world, thus rendering possible a priori synthetic propositions on which all knowledge of a system of nature rests.

The practical use of ordinary human reason confirms the correctness of this deduction. When we present examples of honesty of purpose, of steadfastness in following good maxims, and of sympathy and general benevolence even with great sacrifices of advantage and comfort, there is no man, not even the most malicious villain (provided he is otherwise accustomed to using his reason), who does not wish that he also might have these qualities, but because of his inclinations and impulses cannot bring this about, yet at the same time wishes to be free from such inclinations which are burdensome even to him. He thus proves that with a will free from all impulses of sensibility, he in thought transfers himself into an order of things altogether different from that of his desires in the field of sensibility. He cannot expect to obtain by that wish any gratification of desires or any state which would satisfy his actual or even imagined inclinations, for the Idea itself, which elicits this wish from him, would lose its preeminence if he had any such expectation. He imagines himself to be this better person when he transfers himself to the standpoint of a member of the intelligible world to which he is involuntarily impelled by the Idea of freedom (i.e., of independence from the determining causes in the world of sense); and from this standpoint he is conscious of a good will, which on his own confession constitutes the law for his bad will as a member of the world of sense. He acknowledges the authority of the law even while he transgresses it. The moral "ought" is therefore his own

455

volition as a member of the intelligible world, and it is conceived by him as an "ought" only insofar as he regards himself at the same time as a member of the world of sense.

On the Extreme Boundary of All Practical Philosophy

In respect to their will, all men think of themselves as free. Hence arise all judgments of acts as being such as ought to have been done, although they were not done. But this freedom is not an empirical concept and cannot be such, for it continues to hold even though experience shows the contrary of the demands which are necessarily conceived to be consequences of the supposition of freedom. On the other hand it is equally necessary that everything that happens should be inexorably determined by natural laws, and this natural necessity is likewise no empirical concept because it implies the concept of necessity and thus of a priori knowledge. But this concept of a system of nature is confirmed by experience, and it is inevitably presupposed if experience, which is knowledge of the objects of the sense interconnected by universal laws, is to be possible. Therefore freedom is only an Idea of reason whose objective reality in itself is doubtful, while nature is a concept of the understanding which shows and must necessarily show its reality by examples of experience.

There now arises a dialectic of reason, since the freedom ascribed to the will seems to stand in contradiction to natural necessity. At this parting of the ways reason in its speculative aspect finds the path of natural necessity more well-beaten and usable than that of freedom, but in its practical aspect the 456 path of freedom is the only one on which it is possible to make use of reason in our conduct. Hence it is as impossible for the subtlest philosophy as for the commonest reasoning to argue freedom away. Philosophy must therefore assume that no true contradiction will be found between freedom and natural necessity in the same human actions, for it cannot give up the concept of nature any more than that of freedom.

Hence if we should never be able to conceive how freedom is possible, at least this apparent contradiction must be convincingly eradicated. For if even the thought of freedom contradicted itself or nature, it would have to be surrendered in competition with natural necessity.

But it would be impossible to escape this contradiction if the subject, who seems to himself to be free, thought of himself in the same sense or in the same relationship when he calls himself free as when he assumes that in the same action he is subject to natural law. Therefore it is an inescapable task of speculative philosophy to show at least that its illusion of contradiction rests on the fact that we [do not] think of man in a different sense and relationship when we call him free from that in which we consider him as part of nature and subject to its laws. It must show not only that they can very well coexist but also that they must be thought of as necessarily united in one and the same subject; for otherwise no ground could be given as to why we should burden reason with an Idea which, though it may without contradiction be united with another that is sufficiently established, nevertheless involves us in a perplexity which sorely embarrasses reason in its theoretical use. This duty is imposed only on theoretical philosophy, so that it may clear the way for practical philosophy. Thus the philosopher has no choice as to whether he will remove the apparent contradiction or leave it untouched, for in the latter case the theory of it would be unoccupied land, into the possession of which the fatalist could rightly enter and drive all morality from its alleged property as occupying it without title.

Yet we cannot say here that we have reached the boundary of practical philosophy. For the settlement of the controversy does not belong to practical philosophy, as the latter only 457 demands from theoretical reason that it put an end to the discord in which it entangles itself in theoretical questions, so that practical reason may have rest and security from outward attacks which could dispute it the ground on which it desires to erect its edifice.

The title to freedom of the will claimed by ordinary reason

is based on the consciousness and the conceded presupposition of the independence of reason from merely subjectively determining causes which together constitute what belongs only to sensation and is included under the general name of sensibility. Man, who in this way regards himself as intelligence, puts himself in a different order of things and in a relationship to determining grounds of an altogether different kind when he thinks of himself as intelligence with a will and thus as endowed with causality, compared with that other order of things and that other set of determining grounds which become relevant when he perceives himself as a phenomenon in the world of sense (as he really is also) and submits his causality to external determination according to natural laws. Now he soon realizes that both can subsist together—indeed, that they must. For there is not the least contradiction between a thing in appearance (as belonging to the world of sense) being subject to certain laws from which, as a thing or being regarded as it is in itself, it is independent. That he must think of himself in this twofold manner rests, with regard to the first, on the consciousness of himself as an object affected through the senses, and, with regard to what is required by the second, on the consciousness of himself as intelligence (i.e., as independent of sensible impressions in the use of reason), and thus as belonging to the intelligible world.

This is why man claims to possess a will which does not make him accountable for what belongs only to his desires and inclinations, but thinks of actions which can be done only by disregarding all his desires and sensuous attractions as possible and indeed as necessary for him. The causality of these actions lies in him as an intelligence and in effects and actions in accordance with principles of an intelligible world, of which he knows only that reason alone, and indeed pure reason independent of sensibility, gives the law in it. Moreover, since it is only as intelligence that he is his proper self (as man he is only appearance of himself), he knows that those laws apply to him directly and categorically, so that that to which inclinations and impulses and hence the entire nature of the world of sense incite him cannot in the least impair the laws of his volition as an intelligence. He does not even hold himself responsible for these inclinations and impulses or attribute them to his proper self (i.e., his will), though he does impute to his will the indulgence which he may grant to them when he permits them to influence his maxims to the detriment of the rational laws of his will.

When practical reason thinks itself into an intelligible world, it does in no way transcend its boundaries. It would do so, however, if it tried to intuit or feel itself into it. The intelligible world is only a negative thought with respect to the world of sense, which does not give reason any laws for determining the will. It is positive only in the single point that freedom as negative determination is at the same time connected with a positive power and even a causality of reason. This causality we call a will to act so that the principle of actions will accord with the essential characteristic of a rational cause (i.e., with the condition of universal validity of a maxim as law). But if it were to borrow an object of the will (i.e., a motive) from the intelligible world, it would overstep its boundaries and pretend to be acquainted with something of which it knows nothing. The concept of a world of understanding is therefore only a standpoint from which reason sees itself forced to take outside appearances, in order to think of itself as practical. If the influences of sensibility were determining for man, this would not be possible; but it is necessary unless he is to be denied the consciousness of himself as an intelligence, and thus as a rational and rationally active cause (i.e., a cause acting in freedom). This thought certainly implies the Idea of an order and legislation different from that of natural mechanism, which applies to the world of sense; and it makes necessary the concept of an intelligible world, the whole of rational beings as things regarded as they are in themselves. But it does not give us the least occasion to think of it otherwise than according to its formal condition only (i.e., the universality of the maxim of the will as law and thus the autonomy of the will), which alone is consistent with freedom. All laws, on the other hand, which are directed to an object make for heteronomy, which belongs only to natural laws and which can apply only to the world of sense.

But reason would overstep its bounds if it undertook to explain how pure reason can be practical, which is the same problem as explaining how freedom is possible. 459

We can explain nothing but what we can reduce to laws whose object can be given in some possible experience. But freedom is only an Idea, the objective reality which can in no way be shown to accord with natural laws or to be in any possible experience. Since no example in accordance with any analogy can support it, it can never be comprehended or even imagined. It holds only as the necessary presupposition of reason in a being who believes himself conscious of a will (i.e., of a faculty different from the mere faculty of desire, or a faculty of determining himself to act as an intelligence and thus according to laws of reason independently of natural instincts. But where determination according to natural laws comes to an end, there too all explanation ceases, and nothing remains but defense (i.e., refutation of the objections from those who pretend to have seen more deeply into the essence of things and who boldly declare freedom to be impossible). We can show them only that the supposed contradiction they have discovered lies nowhere else than in their necessarily regarding man [only] as appearance in order to make natural law valid with respect to human actions, and now when we require them to think of man *qua* intelligence as a thing regarded as it is in itself, they still persist in considering him as appearance [only]. Obviously, then, the detachment of his causality (his will) from all natural laws of the world of sense in one and the same subject is a contradiction, but this disappears when they reconsider and confess, as is reasonable, that behind the appearances things regarded as they are in themselves must stand as their hidden ground, and that we cannot expect the laws of the activity of these grounds to be the same as those under which their appearances stand.

The subjective impossibility of explaining the freedom of the will is the same as the impossibility of discovering and explaining an interest* which man can take in moral laws. Nevertheless, he does actually take an interest in them, and the foundation of this interest in us we will call the moral feeling. This moral feeling has been erroneously construed by some as the standard for our moral judgment, whereas it must be regarded rather as the subjective effect which the law has upon the will to which reason alone gives objective grounds.

In order to will an action which reason alone prescribes to the sensuously affected rational being as the action which he ought to will, there is certainly required a power of will to instill a feeling of pleasure of satisfaction in the fulfilment of duty, and hence there must be a causality of reason to determine sensibility in accordance with its own principles. But it is wholly impossible to discern, i.e., to make a priori conceivable, how a mere thought containing nothing sensuous is able to produce a sensation of pleasure or displeasure. For that is a particular kind of causality of which, as of all causality, we cannot determine anything a priori but must consult experience only. But since experience can exemplify the relation of cause to effect only as subsisting between two objects of experience, while here pure reason by mere Ideas (which furnish no object for experience) is to be the cause of an effect which does lie within experience, an explanation of

459   *Interest is that by which reason becomes practical (i.e., a cause determining the will). We therefore say only of a rational being that he takes an interest in something; irrational creatures feel only sensuous impulses. A direct interest in the action is taken by reason only if the universal validity of its maxim is a sufficient determining ground of the will. Only such an interest is pure. But if reason can determine the will only by means of another object of desire or under the presupposition of a particular feeling of the subject, reason takes merely an indirect interest in the action, and since reason for itself alone without experience can discover neither objects of the will nor a particular feeling which lies at its root, that indirect interest would be only empirical and not a pure interest of reason. The logical interest of reason in advancing its insights is never direct but rather presupposes purposes for which they are to be used.

how and why the universality of the maxim as law (and hence morality) interests us is completely impossible for us men. Only this much is certain: that it is valid for us not because it interests us (for that is heteronomy and dependence of practical reason on sensibility, i.e., on a basic feeling; and thus it could never be morally legislating); but that it interests us because it is valid for us as men, inasmuch as it has arisen from our will as intelligence and hence from our proper self; but what belongs to mere appearance is necessarily subordinated to the character of the thing regarded as it is in itself.

461

Thus the question *How is a categorical imperative possible?* can be answered to this extent: We can cite the only presupposition under which it is possible. This is the Idea of freedom, and we can have insight into the necessity of this presupposition which is sufficient to the practical use of reason (i.e., to the conviction of the validity of this imperative and hence also of the moral law). But how this presupposition itself is possible can never be discerned by any human reason. However, on the presupposition of freedom of the will as an intelligence, its autonomy as the formal condition under which alone it can be determined is a necessary consequence. To presuppose the freedom of the will is not only quite possible, as speculative philosophy itself can prove, for it does not involve itself in a contradiction with the principle of natural necessity in the interconnection of appearances in the world of sense. But it is also unconditionally necessary that a rational being conscious of its causality through reason, and thus conscious of a will different from desires, should practically presuppose freedom (i.e., presuppose it in the Idea as the fundamental condition of all his voluntary acts). Yet how pure reason, without any other incentives whencesoever derived, can by itself be practical (i.e., how the simple principle of the universal validity of its maxims as laws — which would certainly be the form of a pure practical reason — without any material (object) of the will in which we might in advance take some interest), and can itself furnish an incentive and produce an interest which would be called purely moral; or, in other words, *how pure reason can be practical*

—to explain this, all human reason is wholly incompetent, and all the pain and work of seeking an explanation of it are wasted.

462 It is just the same as if I sought to find out how freedom itself as the causality of a will is possible, for in so doing I would leave the philosophical basis of explanation behind, and I have no other. Certainly I could revel in the intelligible world, the world of intelligences, which still remains to me; but although I have a well-founded Idea of it, still I do not have the least knowledge of it, nor can I ever attain knowledge of it by all the exertions of my natural faculty of reason. This intelligible world signifies only a something which remains when I have excluded from the determining grounds of my will everything belonging to the world of sense, in order to isolate the principle of motives from the field of sensibility. I do so by limiting it and showing that it does not contain absolutely everything in itself but that outside it there is still more; but this more I do not know. After banishing all material (i.e., knowledge of objects) from pure reason which formulates this ideal, there remain to me only the form, the practical law of the universal validity of maxims, and, in accordance with this, reason in relation to a pure intelligible world as a possible efficient cause determining the will. Any incentive must here be totally absent unless this Idea of an intelligible world or that in which reason directly takes an interest be the incentive. But to make this conceivable is precisely the problem we cannot solve.

Here, then, is the outermost boundary of all moral inquiry. To define it is very important, both in order that reason may not seek around, on the one hand, in the world of sense, in a way harmful to morals, for the supreme motive and for a comprehensible but empirical interest; and so that it will not, on the other hand, impotently flap its wings in the space (for it, an empty space) of transcendent concepts which we call the intelligible world, without being able to move from its starting point and so losing itself amid phantoms. Furthermore, the Idea of a pure intelligible world as a whole of all intelligences to which we ourselves belong as rational beings (though on the other side we are at the same time members of the world of sense) is always a useful and permissible Idea for the purpose of a rational faith. This is so even though all knowledge terminates at its boundary, for the glorious ideal of a universal realm of ends regarded as they are in themselves (rational beings) can awaken in us a lively interest in the moral law. To that realm we can belong as members only 463 when we scrupulously conduct ourselves by maxims of freedom as if they were laws of nature.

Concluding Remark

The speculative use of reason with respect to nature leads to the absolute necessity of some supreme cause of the world. The practical use of reason with respect to freedom leads also to an absolute necessity, but to the necessity only of laws of actions of a rational being as such. Now it is an essential principle of all use of reason to push its knowledge to an awareness of its necessity, for otherwise it would not be rational knowledge. But it is also an equally essential restriction of this very same reason that it cannot discern the necessity of what is or of what occurs or of what ought to be done unless a condition under which it is or occurs or ought to be done is presupposed. In this way, however, the satisfaction of reason is only postponed further and further by the unceasing search for the condition. Reason, therefore, restlessly seeking the unconditionally necessary, sees itself compelled to assume it though it has no means by which to make it comprehensible; it is happy enough if it can discover only the concept which is compatible with this presupposition. It is, therefore, no objection to our deduction of the supreme principle of morality, but a reproach that we must make to human reason generally, that it cannot render comprehensible the absolute necessity of an unconditional practical law (such as the categorical imperative must be). Reason cannot be blamed for being unwilling to explain it by a condition (i.e., by making some interest its basis), for then the law would cease to be moral and would no longer be the supreme law of freedom. And so we do not indeed comprehend the unconditional practical necessity of the moral imperative; yet we do comprehend its incomprehensibility, which is all that can fairly be demanded of a philosophy which in its principles strives to reach the boundary of human reason.

 # WHAT IS ENLIGHTENMENT?

Enlightenment is man's release from his self-incurred tutelage. Tutelage is man's inability to make use of his understanding without direction from another. Self-incurred is this
tutelage when its cause lies not in lack of reason but in lack of
resolution and courage to use it without direction from another. *Sapere aude!** "Have courage to use your own
reason!"—that is the motto of enlightenment.

Laziness and cowardice are the reasons why so great a
portion of mankind, after nature has long since discharged
them from external direction (*naturaliter maiorennes*), nevertheless remain under lifelong tutelage, and why it is so
easy for others to set themselves up as their guardians. It is so
easy not to be of age. If I have a book which understands for
me, a pastor who has a conscience for me, a physician who
decides my diet, and so forth, I need not trouble myself. I
need not think, if I can only pay—others will readily undertake the irksome work for me.

That the step to competence is held be very dangerous by
the far greater portion of mankind (and by the entire fair
sex)—quite apart from its being arduous—is seen to by
those guardians who have so kindly assumed superintend-
ence over them. After the guardians have first made their
domestic cattle dumb and have made sure that these placid
creatures will not dare take a single step without the harness
of the cart to which they are tethered, the guardians then
show them the danger which threatens if they try to go
alone. Actually, however, this danger is not so great, for by
falling a few times they would finally learn to walk alone. But
an example of this failure makes them timid and ordinarily
frightens them away from all further trials.

* "Dare to be wise!" (Horace *Ars poetica*). This was the motto adopted
by the Society of the Friends of Truth, an important circle in the German
Enlightenment.

For any single individual to work himself out of the life under tutelage which has become almost his nature is very difficult. He has come to be fond of this state, and he is for the present really incapable of making use of his reason, for no one has ever let him try it out. Statutes and formulas, those mechanical tools of the rational employment or rather mis-employment of his natural gifts, are the fetters of an everlasting tutelage. Whoever throws them off makes only an uncertain leap over the narrowest ditch because he is not accustomed to that kind of free motion. Therefore, there are few who have succeeded by their own exercise of mind both in freeing themselves from incompetence and in achieving a steady pace.

But that the public should enlighten itself is more possible; indeed, if only freedom is granted, enlightenment is almost sure to follow. For there will always be some independent thinkers, even among the established guardians of the great masses, who, after throwing off the yoke of tutelage from their own shoulders, will disseminate the spirit of the rational appreciation of both their own worth and every man's vocation for thinking for himself. But be it noted that the public, which has first been brought under this yoke by their guardians, forces the guardians themselves to remain bound when it is incited to do so by some of the guardians who are themselves incapable of any enlightenment — so harmful is it to implant prejudices, for they later take vengeance on their cultivators or on their descendants. Thus the public can only slowly attain enlightenment. Perhaps a fall of personal despotism or of avaricious or tyrannical oppression may be accomplished by revolution, but never a true reform in ways of thinking. Rather, new prejudices will serve as well as old ones to harness the great unthinking masses.

For this enlightenment, however, nothing is required but freedom, and indeed the most harmless among all the things to which this term can properly be applied. It is the freedom to make public use of one's reason at every point.* But I hear

---

* It is this freedom Kant claimed later in his conflict with the censor, deferring to the censor in the "private" use of reason, i.e., in his lectures.

on all sides, "Do not argue!" The officer says: "Do not argue but drill!" The tax collector: "Do not argue but pay!" The cleric: "Do not argue but believe!" Only one prince in the world says, "Argue as much as you will, and about what you will, but obey!" Everywhere there is restriction on freedom.

Which restriction is an obstacle to enlightenment, and which is not an obstacle but a promoter of it? I answer: The public use of one's reason must always be free, and it alone can bring about enlightenment among men. The private use of reason, on the other hand, may often be very narrowly restricted without particularly hindering the progress of enlightenment. By the public use of one's reason I understand the use which a person makes of it as a scholar before the reading public. Private use I call that which one may make of it in a particular civil post or office which is entrusted to him. Many affairs which are conducted in the interest of the community require a certain mechanism through which some members of the community must passively conduct themselves with an artificial unanimity, so that the government may direct them to public ends, or at least prevent them from destroying those ends. Here argument is certainly not allowed—one must obey. But so far as a part of the mechanism regards himself at the same time as a member of the whole community or of a society of world citizens, and thus in the role of a scholar who addresses the public (in the proper sense of the word) through his writings, he certainly can argue without hurting the affairs for which he is in part responsible as a passive member. Thus it would be ruinous for an officer in service to quibble about the suitability or utility of a command given to him by his superior; he must obey. But the right to make remarks on errors in the military service and to lay them before the public for judgment cannot equitably be refused him as a scholar. The citizen cannot refuse to pay the taxes imposed on him; indeed, an impudent complaint at those levied on him can be punished as a scandal (as it could occasion general refractoriness). But the same person nevertheless does not act contrary to his duty as a citizen when, as a scholar, he publicly expresses his thoughts on the inappropriateness or even the injustice of these levies. Similarly a cler- 38

gyman is obligated to make his sermon to his pupils in cate-
chism and his congregation conform to the symbol of the
church which he serves, for he has been accepted on this
condition. But as a scholar he has complete freedom, even
the calling, to communicate to the public all his carefully
tested and well-meaning thoughts on that which is erroneous
in the symbol and to make suggestions for the better organization of the religious body and church. In doing this there is
nothing that could be laid as a burden on his conscience. For
what he teaches as a consequence of his office as a represent-
ative of the church, this he considers something about which
he has no freedom to teach according to his own lights; it is
something which he is appointed to propound at the dictation
of and in the name of another. He will say, "Our church
teaches this or that; those are the proofs which it adduces."
He thus extracts all practical uses for his congregation from
statutes to which he himself would not subscribe with full
conviction but to the enunciation of which he can very well
pledge himself because it is not impossible that truth lies
hidden in them, and, in any case, there is at least nothing in
them contradictory to inner religion. For if he believed he
had found such in them, he could not conscientiously dis-
charge the duties of his office; he would have to give it up.
The use, therefore, which an appointed teacher makes of his
reason before his congregation is merely private, because this
congregation is only a domestic one (even if it be a large
gathering); with respect to it, as a priest, he is not free, nor
can he be free, because he carries out the orders of another.
But as a scholar, whose writings speak to his public, the
world, the clergyman in the public use of his reason enjoys an
unlimited freedom to use his own reason and to speak in his
own person. That the guardians of the people (in spiritual
things) should themselves be incompetent is an absurdity
which amounts to the eternalization of absurdities.

But would not a society of clergymen, perhaps a church
conference or a venerable classis (as they call themselves
among the Dutch), be justified in obligating itself by oath to a
certain unchangeable symbol in order to enjoy an unceasing
guardianship over each of its members and thereby over the

people as a whole, and even to make it eternal? I answer that 39
this is altogether impossible. Such a contract, made to shut off
all further enlightenment from the human race, is absolutely
null and void even if confirmed by the supreme power, by
parliaments, and by the most ceremonious of peace treaties.
An age cannot bind itself and ordain to put the succeeding
one into such a condition that it cannot extend its (at best
very occasional) knowledge, purify itself of errors, and progress in general enlightenment. That would be a crime
against human nature, the proper destination of which lies
precisely in this progress; and the descendants would be fully
justified in rejecting those decrees as having been made in an
unwarranted and malicious manner.

The touchstone of everything that can be concluded as a
law for a people lies in the question whether the people
could have imposed such a law on itself. Now such a religious
compact might be possible for a short and definitely limited
time, as it were, in expectation of a better. One might let
every citizen, and especially the clergyman, in the role of
scholar, make his comments freely and publicly, i.e., through
writing, on the erroneous aspects of the present institution.
The newly introduced order might last until insight into the
nature of these things had become so general and widely
approved that through uniting their voices (even if not unani-
mously) they could bring a proposal to the throne to take
those congregations under protection which had united into a
changed religious organization according to their better
ideas, without, however, hindering others who wish to remain in the older. But to unite in a permanent religious
institution which is not to be subject to doubt before the
public even in the lifetime of one man, and thereby to make a
period of time fruitless in the progress of mankind toward
improvement, thus working to the disadvantage of posterity
—that is absolutely forbidden. For himself (and only for a
short time) a man may postpone enlightenment in what he
ought to know, but to renounce it for himself and even more
to renounce it for posterity is to injure and trample on the
rights of mankind.

And what a people may not decree for itself can even less 40 be decreed for them by a monarch, for his lawgiving authority rests on his uniting the general public will in his own. If he only sees to it that all true or alleged improvement stands together with civil order, he can leave it to his subjects to do what they find necessary for their spiritual welfare. This is not his concern, though it is incumbent on him to prevent one of them from violently hindering another in determining and promoting this welfare to the best of his ability. To meddle in these matters lowers his own majesty, since by the writings in which his subjects seek to present their views he may evaluate his own governance. He can do this when, with deepest understanding, he lays open himself the reproach, *Caesar non est supra grammaticos.* Far more does he injure his own majesty when he degrades his supreme power by supporting the ecclesiastical despotism of some tyrants in his state over his other subjects.

If we are asked, "Do we now live in an *enlightened age?*" the answer is, "No," but we do live in an *age of enlightenment.* As things now stand, much is lacking which prevents men from being, or easily becoming, capable of correctly using their own reason in religious matters with assurance and free from outside direction. But, on the other hand, we have clear indications that the field has now been opened wherein men may freely deal with these things and that the obstacles to general enlightenment or the release from self-imposed tutelage are gradually being reduced. In this respect, this is the age of enlightenment, or the century of Frederick.

A prince who does not find it unworthy of himself to say that he holds it to be his duty to prescribe nothing to men in religious matters but to give them complete freedom while renouncing the haughty name of *tolerance*, is himself enlightened and deserves to be esteemed by the grateful world and posterity as the first, at least from the side of government, who divested the human race of its tutelage and left each man free to make use of his reason in matters of conscience. Under him venerable ecclesiastics are allowed, in the role of scholars and without infringing on their official duties, freely to submit for public testing their judgments and views which here and there diverge from the established symbol. And an even greater freedom is enjoyed by those who are restricted by no official duties. This spirit of freedom spreads beyond this land, even to those in which it must struggle with external obstacles erected by a government that misunderstands its own interest. For an example gives evidence to such a government that in freedom there is not the least cause for concern about public peace and the stability of the community. Men work themselves gradually out of barbarity if only intentional artifices are not made to hold them in it.

I have placed the main point of enlightenment—the escape of men from their self-incurred tutelage—chiefly in matters of religion because our rulers have no interest in playing the guardian with respect to the arts and sciences and also because religious immaturity is not only the most harmful but also the most degrading of all. But the manner of thinking of the head of a state who favors religious enlightenment goes farther, and sees that there is no danger to his sovereignty in allowing his subjects to make public use of their reason and to publish their thoughts on better formulation of his legislation and even their open-minded criticisms of the laws already made. Of this we have a shining example wherein no monarch is superior to him whom we honor.

But only he who, himself enlightened, is not afraid of shadows, and who has a numerous and well-disciplined army to assure public peace, can say: "Argue as much as you will, and about what you will, only obey!" A republic could not dare say such a thing. Here is shown a strange and unexpected trend in human affairs in which almost everything, looked at in the large, is paradoxical. A greater degree of civil freedom appears advantageous to the freedom of mind of the people, and yet it places inescapable limitations upon it; a lower degree of civil freedom, on the contrary, provides the mind with room for each man to extend himself to his full capacity. As nature has uncovered from under this hard shell the seed for which she most tenderly cares—the propensity and vocation to free thinking—this gradually works back upon the character of the people, who thereby stepwise become capable of managing freedom; finally, it affects the principles of government, which finds it to its advantage to treat men, who are now more than machines, in accordance with their dignity.*

I. KANT

KÖNIGSBERG, PRUSSIA
September 30, 1784

---

*Today I read in the *Büschingsche Wöchentliche Nachrichten* for September 13 an announcement of the *Berlinische Monatsschrift* for this month, which cites the answer to the same question by Herr Mendelssohn. But this issue has not yet come to me; if it had, I would have held back the present essay, which is now put forth only in order to see how much agreement in thought can be brought about by chance.

Moses Mendelssohn's answer was that enlightenment lay in intellectual cultivation, which he distinguished from the practical. Kant refuses to make this distinction fundamental. A study of the political background and occasion for these essays will be found in James Schmidt, "The Question of Enlightenment: Kant, Mendelssohn, and the *Mittwochsgesellschaft*," *Journal of the History of Ideas*, vol. 50 (1989), pp. 269–92.